THE ›DO IT↘ MESSY APPROACH

THE DO IT MESSY APPROACH

A STEP BY STEP GUIDE FOR **INSTRUCTIONAL DESIGNERS** AND **ONLINE LEARNING DEVELOPERS**

ROBIN SARGENT, PhD

ILLUSTRATED BY JAMES BEVELANDER

Text: Robin Sargent, PhD
Illustrations & Cover: James Bevelander

Independently published in 2022.

ISBN: 979-8-9864814-0-1

Copyright ©2022
All rights reserved.

Robin Sargent, PhD
info@idolcourses.com
www.idolcourses.com

DEDICATION

To all current, aspiring, and future IDOLs™.

CONTENTS

DEDICATION..v

FOREWORD..xi

INTRODUCTION..1

PART 1: Foundations 21

CHAPTER 1: *Who's Your ADDIE?* 23
An Introduction to Instructional Design

CHAPTER 2: *Information is Not Instruction:*....................29
The First Principles of Instruction

CHAPTER 3: *Quick & Dirty:* 47
Your Needs Analysis

CHAPTER 4: *It's Pronounced "Smee":*.............................59
Subject Matter Experts

PART 2: Reverse Engineering Your Blueprint Design 73

CHAPTER 5: *Well, There's Your Problem:*.......................75
Identify a Problem

CHAPTER 6: *Show 'em How It's Done:* 99
Create the Demonstration for the Final Problem Scenario

CHAPTER 7: *Give Your Learners a Turn:* 117
Create the Application for the Final Scenario

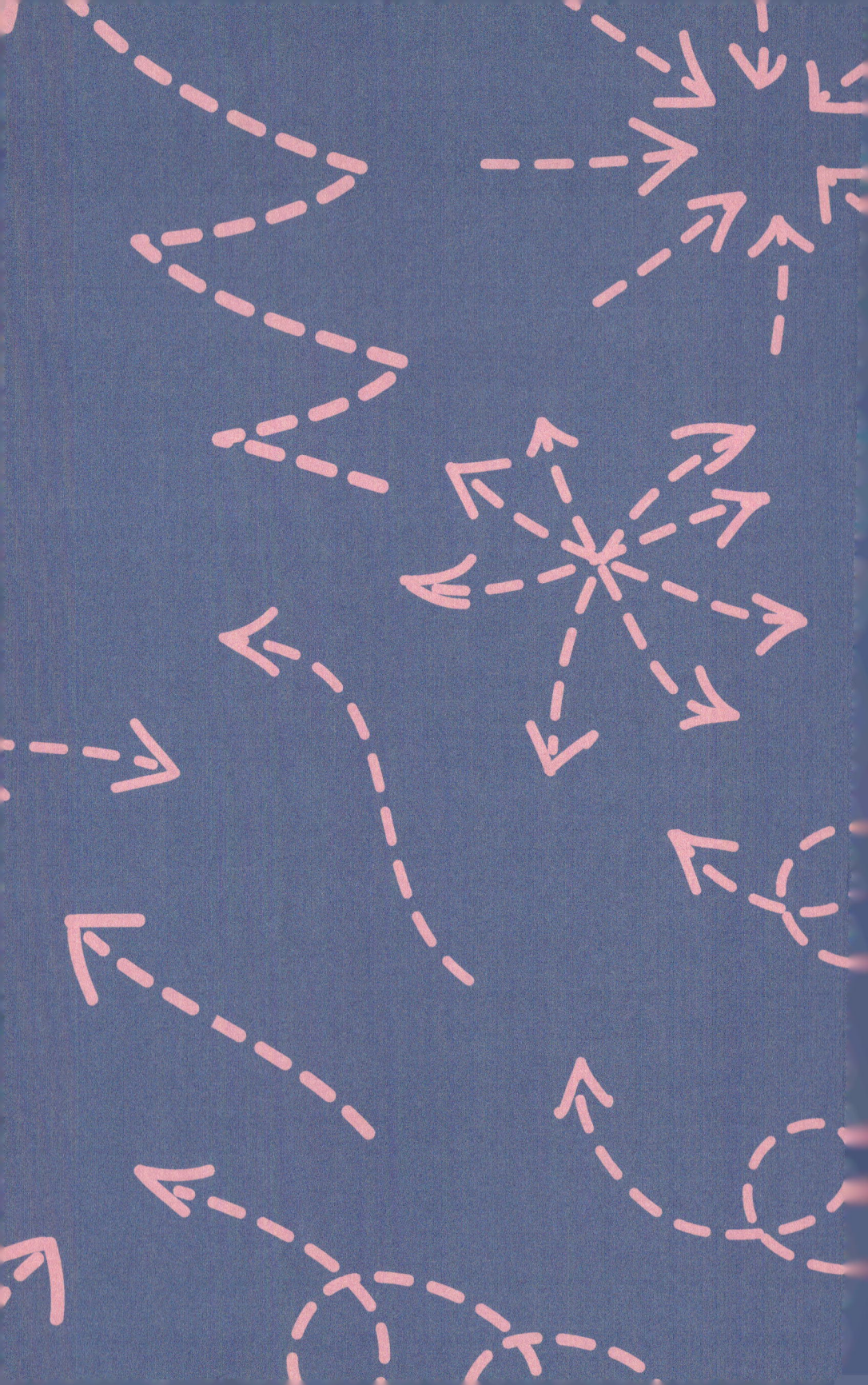

CHAPTER 8: *99 Problems:* 137
Create Several Problem Scenarios

CHAPTER 9: *It's Easy, If It's Not Hard:* 149
Order the Scenarios from Easiest to Hardest

CHAPTER 10: *Show 'Em Again:* 153
Create a Demonstration for Problems 1–2

CHAPTER 11: *Practice Makes Permanent:* 173
Create an Application for Problems 3–5

CHAPTER 12: *End of the Line:* 191
Create an Application for Problems 6–8
that Provides No Guidance

CHAPTER 13: *Hide & Seek:* 211
Identify the Component Skills

CHAPTER 14: *Show What You Know:* 221
Assessment Design

CHAPTER 15: *Check & Double-Check:* 229
Review Each Problem Set

PART 3: Enhancement & Next Steps 259

CHAPTER 16: *Integato Enhanceum:* 261
Integration & Enhancement Strategies

CHAPTER 17: *There is No Failure, Only Feedback:* 273
Get Feedback

CHAPTER 18: Further Research & Resources 279

FURTHER READING 293

ABOUT THE AUTHOR 297

FOREWORD

THE INSTRUCTIONAL DESIGN world is changing right before our very eyes. Every day, I am still completely shocked to hear about how many people want to become instructional designers. Don't get me wrong, this isn't a bad thing! It's actually the opposite; I think this is a wonderful change! I love instructional design, even if my own start was a bit rocky. You see, it took me years to become an instructional designer. Back in 2016, no one seemed to know what instructional designers actually did and what value we can bring to projects. It felt like we were in a secret club, and only other instructional designers understood the joys and hardships of the role.

My first assignment as an instructional designer was terrifying, to put it mildly. The university I worked at was known for creating partnerships with well-known, massive organizations. Together, they would create a learning environment that provided both academic and practical on-the-job lessons to design an optimal learning experience. While I had fantastic mentors, I still felt like a fish out of water. Each day, I woke up nervous, thinking that I was doing something incorrectly simply because I had no idea about how to do the job. I knew how learning works, but other than that, I didn't have a clue about the day-to-day activities of a designer. I learned through trial and error (mostly error) about topics such as conducting needs analysis, managing a project, creating a blueprint, collaborating with subject matter experts, and designing for how adults learn. While I wouldn't change a thing about my own instructional design journey, I did always wonder why there wasn't some form of a simple step-by-step guide when it came to designing online courses and programs. Fast forward from 2016 to today, and Dr. Sargent has written this guide.

What you have in front of you is the guidebook that I wish existed back when I became an instructional designer. I remember when Dr. Sargent and I were talking about this idea for her book. She wanted to bring Dr. David Merrill's teachings to life in a different way. Since Dr. Merrill is literally a living legend in the learning space, I thought it was a fantastic idea to take his First Principles of Instruction and combine them with her own philosophies on instructional design.

In this book, you'll be guided by Dr. Sargent on every step for your projects. Her words are clear and concise to help you grasp the real concepts, and you won't be lost in some academic jargon from a textbook. The focus is on solving problems through education and training, and doing it in a way that will wow your learners. You'll explore the significance of creating real-life scenarios to help your learners retain the necessary information and to make it stick. You'll see resources, templates, and examples to follow and to inspire you. And if you ever have a doubt that you missed a step, you can simply follow the checklists to mark off each item one-by-one. Basically, what I'm trying to say is to follow each part of this book and believe in yourself. You have the tools to teach you the fundamentals and to create the experiences you are hoping for.

DR. LUKE HOBSON
Senior Instructional Designer and Program Manager at MIT
Author of *What I Wish I Knew Before Becoming an Instructional Designer*
Host of the Dr. Luke Hobson Podcast and YouTube Channel

INTRODUCTION

CONGRATULATIONS! If you've picked up this book, you are at least exploring the possibility that perhaps, just maybe, you could become an instructional designer and online learning developer (better known as an IDOL™). In other words, you're here because you're ready to design your very own course.

THE DO IT MESSY APPROACH

And guess what? You're right! Even if you have little or no previous learning design experience, even if you believe you have little or no natural talent, as long as you have a course topic idea, can find something to write with, and can set aside at least 20 minutes a day, you are ready to design an amazing course. In fact, many of my students have built their course blueprints in 30 days or less following my "Do It Messy Approach," and they all started out exactly where you are.

Now, you might be curious about what I mean by "course blueprint." A course blueprint is part of a larger course design package. It is a way for an instructional designer to map out the different aspects of instruction and learning that go into a course. This provides you as the designer an opportunity to articulate and lay out a holistic picture of the course. Course blueprints are helpful for your course design and course revision efforts, as well as for discussions with stakeholders regarding the course and how it solves the knowledge, skills, or attitude gaps. The point of developing a course blueprint is so that you can make appropriate changes and choose a direction before you get too deeply into the details of your course. In other words, before you worry about the visuals, narration, or technology, you need to focus on getting the content right. That's what the Do It Messy Approach will teach you.

Yes, you have found the right book. Yes, you have found the right teacher. But you don't have to take my word for it. Read what an IDOL has to say in her own words:

"Honestly, this was the best investment I ever made in MYSELF. I started slow because I had a child born around the same time as I started my first cohort. The #DoItMessy jumpstart was a game-changer for me. Once I changed my mindset from perfection-oriented to outcomes-oriented and from defeat to triumph,

Introduction

everything fell into place. I took deliberate practice seriously and my goals were achieved in kind." —CASSANDRA ROOT

Welcome to the IDOL world of creative possibilities. This book will teach you an easy method to design instruction for corporate training on *any* topic. The problem or task-centered approach I share here can be applied to solving *any* business problem that includes a knowledge or skills gap. I know these are big claims bursting with enormous promise. You may be skeptical and wonder how I can back up such statements. My experience comes from my PhD in Education specializing in Instructional Design and Online Learning, and also I spent more than 17 years designing and delivering training on everything from lab management to construction protocols to sales processes. Much of what I share in this book comes from those on-the-ground experiences. The simplest way for me to qualify my teaching confidence, however, is to share with you examples of courses designed by my past students, and I've included a ton of these in Part 2 and 3 to guide your own blueprint design. For now, though, you can rest assured that everything I teach here comes directly from methods my students have implemented, tested, and iterated upon.

INSTRUCTIONAL DESIGN AS A LEARNED SKILL

Even though I have a PhD specializing in Instructional Design, you certainly don't need a PhD to design an effective and engaging course. Anyone can learn how to design instruction. In fact, my PhD was actually intended as a retirement plan. I thought that after retiring from a career in corporate, I would become a university president. Instead, I ended up starting my own trade school – an alternative university, if you will – for instructional designers, the IDOL courses Academy™. During the past

THE DO IT MESSY APPROACH

four years, I've taught thousands of students how to design instruction through the IDOL courses Academy, the Become an IDOL Podcast, the IDOL courses YouTube channel, and the IDOL courses website. IDOL courses Academy alumni have designed onboarding for Uber, soft skills for Google, warehouse skills for Amazon, healthcare training for Kaiser Permanente, and compliance training for Walmart. As you can see, this book is really only the tip of the iceberg of everything I have to share with you.

> But here's a secret you won't hear from other instructional design teachers: learning is learning and designing is designing, no matter how much experience you have or who your students are. In other words, instructional design is a learned skill. I know the techniques I share in this book work because I've used them with my own students, and they have used them with their students.

The Do It Messy Approach is different from every other instructional design book you will find. Through experience, I've distilled complex information into a straightforward strategy to help you better understand the sophisticated concepts, academic jargon, and complex learning theories of instructional design. I'll introduce the essential ideas – including Merrill's Pebble-in-the-Pond model and principles of instruction, the ADDIE framework, and the ABCD formula for measuring learning outcomes – in a simple, easy-to-follow way. And because I'm a kid at heart, I won't hold back on any of the fun that permeates learning design at its best.

Introduction

Yes, I have experience as an instructional designer in both higher education and corporate settings, but I'm not here to show you how to create cookie-cutter courses. The lessons in each chapter are designed to give you the basic skill set and formula that will enable you to design courses that showcase your unique skills. Using the lessons in this book, you can create instruction or training for any industry in any style (e.g., gamified, themed, competency based) or medium (e.g., online, in person, via video, interactive eLearning, augmented reality, virtual reality).

Also, in the IDOL courses Academy[SM], I teach the fundamental laws of instructional design:

- Learners come first
- Learning is doing
- Contextualize learning through real-world tasks
- Iterative prototyping is better than abstract design specifications
- A feeling of mastery leads to greater levels of learner motivation

And because I believe in walking my talk, I follow these fundamental laws myself, which means you – the learner – come first. In these pages, you will not only learn a method for designing instruction, you will experience the method yourself. This is powerful stuff!

Again, I firmly believe anyone can learn how to design instruction. Instructional design is a learnable skill, just like reading or writing. All you need is the right formula and permission to do it messy. This book offers you both.

DESIGN THINKING AND THE DO IT MESSY APPROACH

In what follows, I teach you how to design instruction using the same proven, step-by-step method that has worked for all of my students. So what's the method? It's called the Do It Messy Approach to instructional design and it has two essential elements: the beginner's mindset and design thinking.

When you take on a beginner's mindset, you set aside any perfectionist tendencies, make quick decisions in the spirit of experimentation, and develop your course knowing that the result will be a blueprint that you can improve over time, through feedback. This is the strategy designers use.

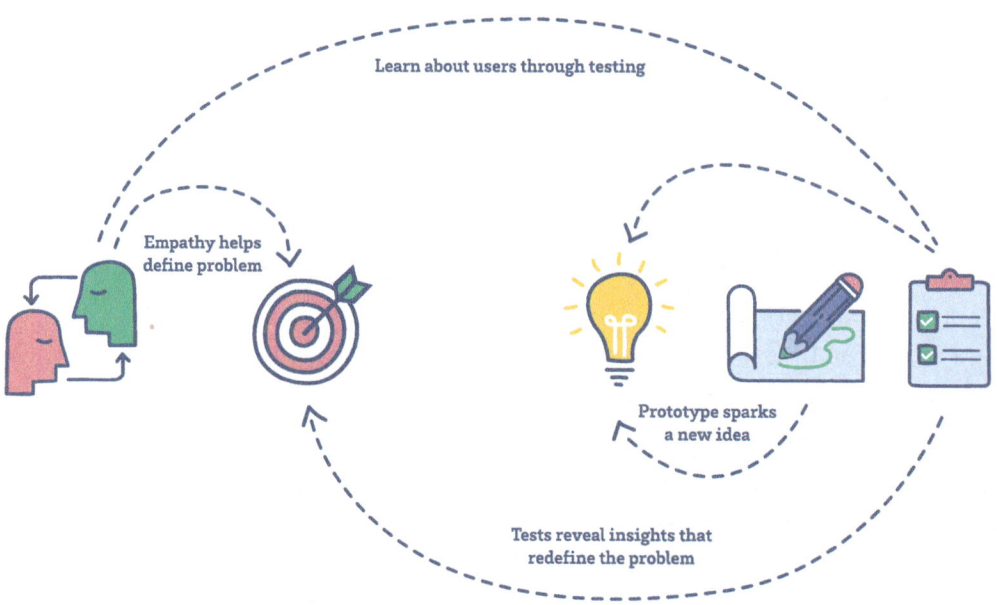

Introduction

With the Do It Messy Approach, you recognize that the design process is "messy" - recursive, iterative - testing blueprints and applying feedback to continually improve. It's not possible to improve what doesn't exist, and lots of people new to the field are reluctant to create an imperfect, incomplete course design. With the Do It Messy Approach, I encourage designers to dive right in and DO IT, understanding that taking action (even imperfect action) is essential to the process.

Learning design projects have phases. In Phase 1, you do a needs analysis, empathize with the learners, and gather vital information about your course project idea. In Phase 2, you define the landscape and acknowledge your constraints. Next comes brainstorming and ideation in Phase 3. Phase 4 is rapid prototyping. And Phase 5 is all about testing and delivering your course. This guide book will lead you through this basic system as you design your course, but it's also important to remember that design thinking is non-linear. This means that you'll develop your course in a different order from how you'll deliver it to your learners.

The Do It Messy Approach trains you to focus on what your learners need to know and the most efficient way to deliver that knowledge. Combining the beginner's mindset with design thinking helps you avoid distractions and get to a complete course blueprint more quickly. From there, you can seek out feedback, iterate on the content you created, add visuals and other enhancement strategies, and continue to improve upon your original design. This is the Do it Messy Approach in a nutshell.

THE FIRST PRINCIPLES OF INSTRUCTION

In addition to being inspired by design thinking, the Do It Messy Approach is influenced by what M. David Merrill calls the "First Principles of Instruction:"[1]

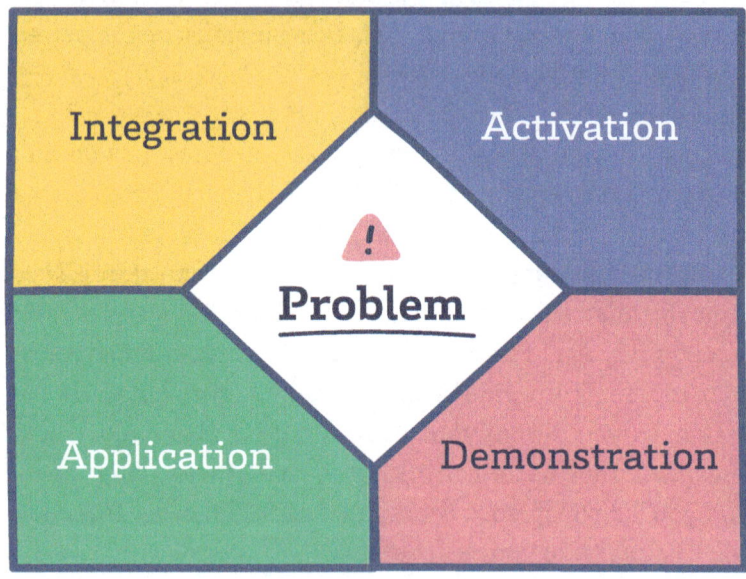

1. The **demonstration** principle: Learning is promoted when learners observe a demonstration.
2. The **application** principle: Learning is promoted when learners apply the new knowledge.
3. The **task-centered** principle: Learning is promoted when learners engage in a task-centered instructional strategy.
4. The **activation** principle: Learning is promoted when learners activate relevant prior knowledge or experience.

---

1 Merrill, M. D. (2009). "First Principles of Instruction." In C. M. Reigeluth & A. Carr (Eds.), *Instructional Design Theories and Models: Building a Common Knowledge Base* (Vol. III). New York: Routledge Publishers.

5. The **integration** principle: Learning is promoted when learners integrate their new knowledge into their everyday world.

I will discuss these first principles along with the basics of instructional design in the first part of the book. Then, in Part 2, you are invited to put these principles to work creating your course blueprint through bite-size, 20-minute lessons. In this way, you will learn the basics, one key term at a time, one step at a time, one problem at a time, then you will apply them to the challenge of building your own course.

THE RIGHT FORMULA

Have you ever taught a kid how to tie their shoes, bake a cake, or catch a fish? If you've ever taught anyone how to do something, then you have some instructional design experience, and the instructions were probably pretty intuitive for you. You simply talk to your learner like they have never tied their own shoes, or baked a cake, or caught a fish by themselves and go through each step, coaching them along the way. Let's stick with the tie your shoe example. When you teach a child to tie their shoes, it might look and sound something like this:

1. "Hey kid! You're getting bigger, so you can learn to tie your own shoes. It's easy! I'll show you how. Do you know how to tie a knot? You do?! That's great, you're going to tie two knots, but you'll include a bow. Let me show you."

THE DO IT MESSY APPROACH

2. "First, you take the two strings, hold them up, cross one over and under the other, then pull them away from each other. That's your first knot! Then you make a loop with each string and do the same thing you just did, but with the loops. Cross the loops, bring one over and under the other, pull them in opposite directions. Ta da! Now it's your turn!"

3. Here is where they take the strings, you give the verbal directions, and maybe you guide their hands on the first attempt or two.

4. Then you tell them it's their turn to do it by themselves. You're still there if they get stuck or have a question, but you aren't holding their hands anymore.

5. Once they've done it on their own, you tell them it's time for them to tie their shoes with no help from you. Maybe you walk into the other room, so you're not tempted to help them in the moment. And what happens? That kid comes and shows you the shoe they tied all by themselves!

Isn't that the best feeling? When you know that little person knows how to do something for the first time and for the rest of their lives because of you and your help. Well, this is exactly what we get to do every day as instructional designers. You may imagine that teaching adult learners job-related skills is more complicated than tying shoes, but we are creating a learning experience that follows the same template.

Next, to make the template that underlies the example clearer, I'll provide the instructional design concepts behind each step. This way, you can see the framework that you can learn and apply to every course design that will result in effective learning, no matter what topic or problem you are dealing with.

Introduction

1. "Hey kid! You're getting bigger, so you can learn to tie your own shoes. It's easy! I'll show you how. Do you know how to tie a knot? You do?! That's great, you're going to tie two knots, but you'll include a bow. Let me show you." **This is what we call ACTIVATION. When you introduce your course you will want to activate and connect your learners' previous knowledge to what you are about to teach them.**

2. "First, you take the two strings, hold them up, cross one over and under the other, then pull them away from each other. That's your first knot! Then you make a loop with each string and do the same thing you just did, but with the loops. Cross the loops, bring one over and under the other, pull them in opposite directions. Ta da! Now it's your turn!" **This is an example of a DEMONSTRATION. When you are designing training you have to show your learners the end result and how to get there. This is something you definitely do intuitively when you are teaching face-to-face, but many struggle to remember to include demonstrations in online learning designs.**

3. Here is where they take the strings, you give the verbal directions, and maybe you guide their hands on the first attempt or two. **Now that you've demonstrated the task, you want your learners to try to do the same. This is called APPLICATION. Since learning to tie your shoes is quite simple and only involves a couple of steps, the application comes rather quickly in this example. Aso notice that during the first application, you are still there to guide, provide feedback, coach, and maybe directly help your learner. You could think of this as a guided application.**

4. Then you tell them it's their turn to do it by themselves. You're still there if they get stuck or have a question,

but you aren't holding their hands anymore. **This is another step in the framework that still falls under APPLICATION. Only this time, you don't hold their hands.** Instead, you let them try to tie their shoes by themselves, while you stand by to answer any question they might have. Or you could provide them with a tie-your-shoes infographic or visual resource they could reference while they try it themselves.

5. Once they've done it on their own, you tell them it's time for them to tie their shoes with no help from you. Maybe you walk into the other room, so you're not tempted to help them in the moment. And what happens? That kid comes and shows you the shoe they tied all by themselves! **This last step is INTEGRATION. The learner gets a chance to take what they've learned and do it all by themselves and implement it in the real world.**

Why did I call out each instructional design concept here and what does teaching a kid how to tie their shoes have to do with corporate instructional design? Well, I wanted to show you that you already have the instincts to design effective training. You've done it before, but it helps to have each piece of the puzzle called out so you can repeat the formula with confidence for every learning experience you create. You've also probably noticed that this formula follows Merrill's First Principles of Instruction. The activation, demonstration, application, and integration formula based on a problem-centered design approach is what you will learn and apply as you read this book.

This is the one framework that combines all of the research, evidence-based practices, and years of instructional design experience into a simple formula that will improve your course designs.

Introduction

So why don't instructional designers everywhere use this formula? Well, some use it by accident as they follow their instincts to design courses. As for the rest, they just don't know about the formula or haven't been exposed to the excellent textbook and research done by M. David Merrill in the book, *First Principles of Instruction*.[2] This is one reason I wanted to write this book. I wanted to create a step-by-step guide for designing course blueprints that integrates all of the best practices and theories in a simple and easy to understand formula.

Here's the basic formula:

Problem-Centered Information
Activation
Demonstration
Application
Integration

---

[2] Merrill, M. D. (2013). *First Principles of Instruction: Identifying and Designing Effective, Efficient, and Engaging Instruction*. San Francisco: Pfeiffer, A Wiley Imprint.

13

THE DO IT MESSY APPROACH

 **TIP**

You can literally use this formula over and over again to design courses that are effective, engaging, and structured.

In fact, we'll follow this model throughout this book.

WHAT'S YOUR COURSE TOPIC OR BUSINESS CHALLENGE?

As you go through this book and apply the lessons, you will have the opportunity to design a full course blueprint of your own. To design your course blueprint, you will obviously need a course topic or business challenge that can be solved with a training solution. So before you begin reading Part 1, you should have in mind a course idea that you want to design.

 **STOP HERE** and figure out your course idea before moving on. If you are brand new to instructional design or don't yet have a topic in mind, choose something either that you know a lot about or that you want to learn well enough to teach someone else.

For a portfolio piece, consider a topic that is applicable to the corporate environment. Tutorial courses such as those on leadership skills, email etiquette, software applications, sales techniques, etc. work well. Or if you have ever written a paper for school that is relevant, you may be able to adapt it into a course.

Introduction

Here is a list of other possible course topics:

- How to create pivot tables in Microsoft Excel
- How to make a budget using Microsoft Excel (or Google Sheets)
- How to merge comments from multiple reviewers in Word
- How to customize the ribbon in any Microsoft Office program
- How to use styles in Microsoft Word for a consistent look
- How to design PowerPoint handouts
- How to create folders to organize Outlook
- How to use filters to make email more efficient
- How to edit out the noise in Audacity
- How to use brushes or filters in Photoshop
- How to organize your team members using a project management tool (Microsoft Project, Basecamp, Trello, ClickUp etc.)
- How to upload a course in an LMS (whichever system you know best)
- How to save links with Diigo, Evernote, or another tool
- How to create consistent file naming conventions for data sets
- Any safety training topics (equipment use and safety, fire safety, cybersecurity and safety, ergonomics in the workplace, etc.)
- A tutorial for any cool trick you know in Captivate, Storyline, or the eLearning development tool of your choice (this also shows your expertise with the tool)

15

THE DO IT MESSY APPROACH

Once you have a topic idea in mind, do some basic research. This might include grabbing stuff from Wikipedia or reading some blogs on the topic. The goal here is to do a brain dump of information about your topic. Of course, if you're starting with a research paper you wrote, you can skip this step.

Now, I've used the term 'blueprint' a few times and shared a basic definition earlier. Still, further explanation may be useful. A blueprint in this context is a text-based document that fleshes out your entire course design. You can think of it in terms of writing a script for your course.

Why design a course blueprint? A blueprint is incredibly useful for someone who is experienced in the field because it gives you a script to share in order to get feedback from colleagues, peers, learners, stakeholders, and subject matter experts (SME) before you spend a lot of time developing a full course that needs significant changes and enhancements. For beginners and those looking to become an IDOL, a blueprint gives you a script upon which to build a portfolio piece or several portfolio pieces, and of course, getting feedback on this blueprint is very valuable at this early stage too.

I've taught a ton of new IDOLs through the IDOL courses Academy[SM] trade school, and what I see new instructional designers struggling with the most is not the analysis of the learners, the training need, or even the technology. Instead, the number one struggle is coming up with the course content. Once you've designed a course blueprint, though, the destination is locked in and all the other logistical pieces fall into place. The heavy-lifting is always in the early stages of figuring out what problem the course solves for learners. My hope is that the Do It Messy Approach will help you get to the problem more quickly, so you can see the component skills and gain the confidence you need to identify all the other pieces of your course project.

HOW TO USE THIS BOOK

This book is divided into three parts. In Part 1, I give you all the background information and concepts you need to know to be able to create your course blueprint. I explain how I understand instructional design (and how I recommend that you understand it too). I break down Merrill's First Principles of Instruction, so that you can see the full picture as you start to envision your course. Then I discuss the roles needs analysis and subject matter experts play in designing your course.

Part 2 is a series of short lessons that you can follow to create your very own course blueprint. Each lesson is designed to be completed in roughly 20 minutes (though some parts may take longer than others, especially if you're brand new to instructional design). Once you have worked your way through each lesson, you'll have a complete course script that you can test, refine, and start using with your own population of learners. Because your goal is to get your course blueprint done, it's important that you put each lesson in Part 2 into action. Don't simply read the chapter. Follow the steps and use the checklists to keep track of your progress.

Finally, Part 3 discusses how to take your course blueprint to the next level. There are integration and enhancement strategies that can help to ensure that your course doesn't simply live on the internet or on your learners' company computers. You want your learners not just to go through the motions, but to truly master the skills you're teaching, and you can develop your ideas beyond this course blueprint as well. In the final chapters, you'll find many resources and suggestions for continuing to build out your course. Remember, this course blueprint you're creating is only the beginning!

Are you ready to put the Do It Messy Approach into practice? Let's do this!

PART ONE
FOUNDATIONS

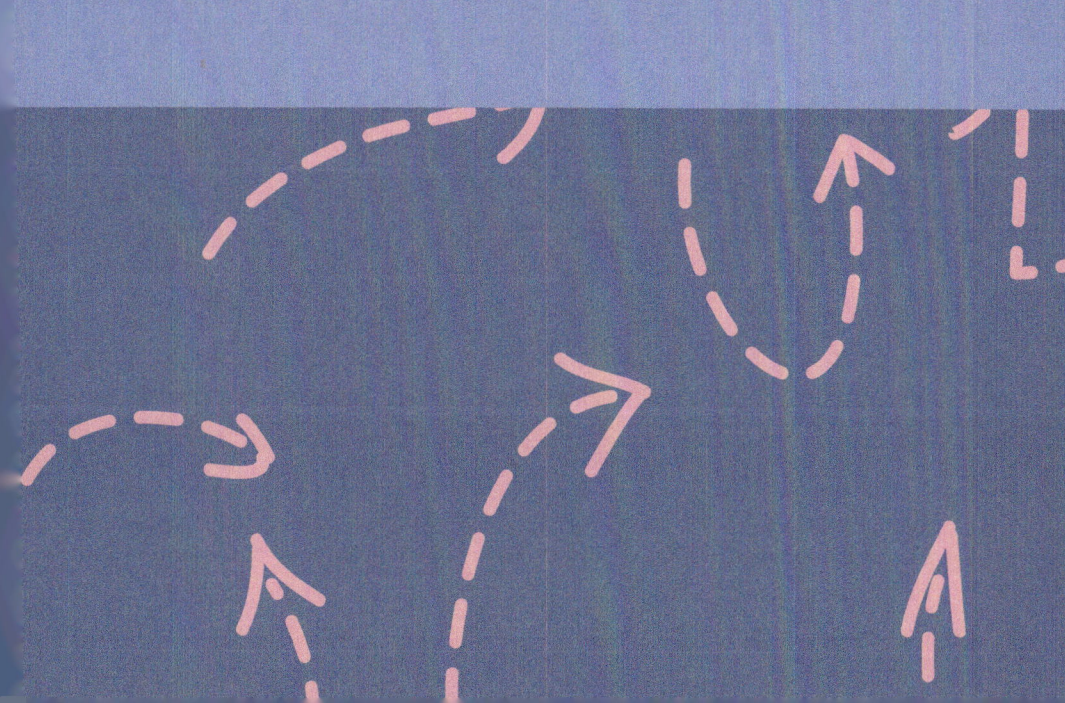

CHAPTER 1

Who's Your ADDIE?

An Introduction to Instructional Design

THE CONCEPT OF INSTRUCTIONAL DESIGN can be traced back to the 1940s. As a field, instructional design has its historical roots in cognitive and behavioral psychology. The idea emerged during a time when behaviorism dominated American psychology and psychologists were researching how to best influence people's behavior. At the same time, systems engineering began to take hold as an interdisciplinary field of engineering. Here, the revolutionary idea that the whole is greater than the sum of its parts gave rise to new methods and modeling techniques that gave people a better understanding of complex engineering systems.[3]

---

3 https://en.wikipedia.org/wiki/Instructional_design

THE DO IT MESSY APPROACH

In addition, early forms of instructional design were linked to the training development model used by the U.S. military. During World War II, for example, military training materials were developed based on the principles of instruction, learning, and human behavior. Following its success in military training, psychologists, like Edgar Dale, B.F. Skinner,[4] and Robert F. Mager[5] began to view training as a system and developed various analysis, design, and evaluation procedures. Various instructional design frameworks later migrated to the industrial sector and to the field of education in the 1950's.

A lot has happened within the field of instructional design since the 1950s, not much of which is relevant for our purposes. Here's what you need to know: Instructional design is about creating learning experiences. It's the process of identifying the performance, skills, knowledge, information, and attitude gaps within a targeted audience and creating, selecting, or suggesting learning experiences that close the gap derived from evidence-based learning theories and best practices from the field.[6] As a definition, this is quite a mouthful. Here it is in plain English: We create learning experiences and solutions to solve business challenges that include knowledge, skill, or attitude gaps.

Whether you've been newly tasked with training employees at your organization or you've been teaching for ages and are interested in finding a new way to reach your learners, instructional design is the skill you're here to sharpen.

---

[4] Skinner, B. F. (1961). "The Science of Learning and the Art of Teaching." In B. F. Skinner, Cumulative Record (pp. 145–157). Appleton-Century-Crofts. https://doi.org/10.1037/11324-010

[5] Mager, R. F. (1961). "On the Sequencing of Instructional Content." *Psychological Reports*. Vol. 9, Issue 2. https://doi.org/10.2466/pr0.1961.9.2.405

[6] https://training.lbl.gov/Resources/InstructionalDesign.html

THE ADDIE FRAMEWORK

There are a wide variety of instructional design models and frameworks available, but one of the most popular is the ADDIE framework. That's why if you've ever formally studied instructional design or were taught by someone with military training, you may be familiar with this concept. A.D.D.I.E. is an acronym that stands for analyze, design, develop, implement, and evaluate.

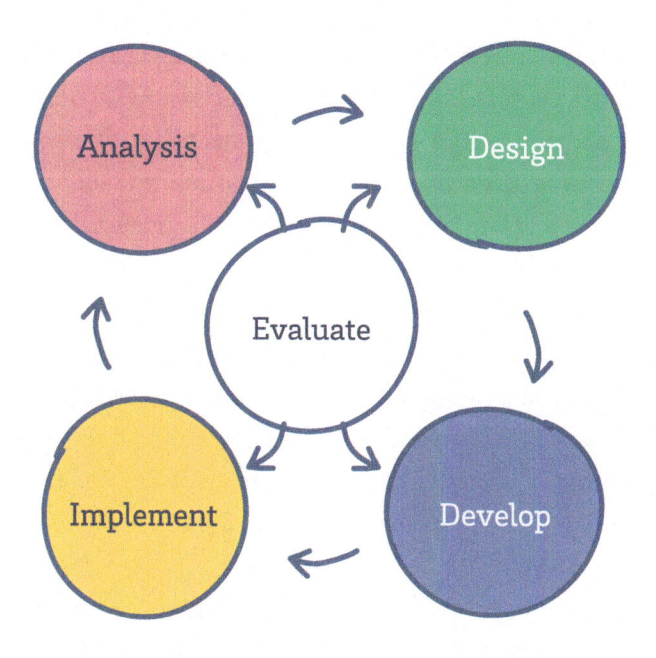

The ADDIE framework:
- Analyze
- Design
- Develop
- Implement
- Evaluate

THE DO IT MESSY APPROACH

As a high level framework for course design, ADDIE can be helpful. Successful instructional designers take time to analyze and determine the needs of their learners, define the end goal of instruction, then design and develop the necessary "intervention" to assist in their learners' transformation. From there, they monitor their learners' implementation of the skills they have been taught and gather the data they need to evaluate and further develop their instructional materials, interventions, or solutions.

However, it's important to recognize the limitations of whatever instructional design process you choose. ADDIE can work well as a structure for completing projects or for improving upon a course after you have your first messy blueprint and beyond, but it offers little direction when it comes to designing the course from the start.

Also, ADDIE reinforces linear thinking and as we know instinctively, learning isn't always a linear process. It's messy! For this reason, I suggest designing your course blueprint using design thinking. That's the basis for the Do It Messy Approach, which I lead you through in Part 2.

Once your blueprint is finished, I encourage you to analyze, re-design, re-develop, implement, and evaluate. Here, at the beginning of developing your blueprint, however, I encourage you to chuck the ADDIE model right out the window.

Here, again, is the basic formula we'll be using in place of the ADDIE model:

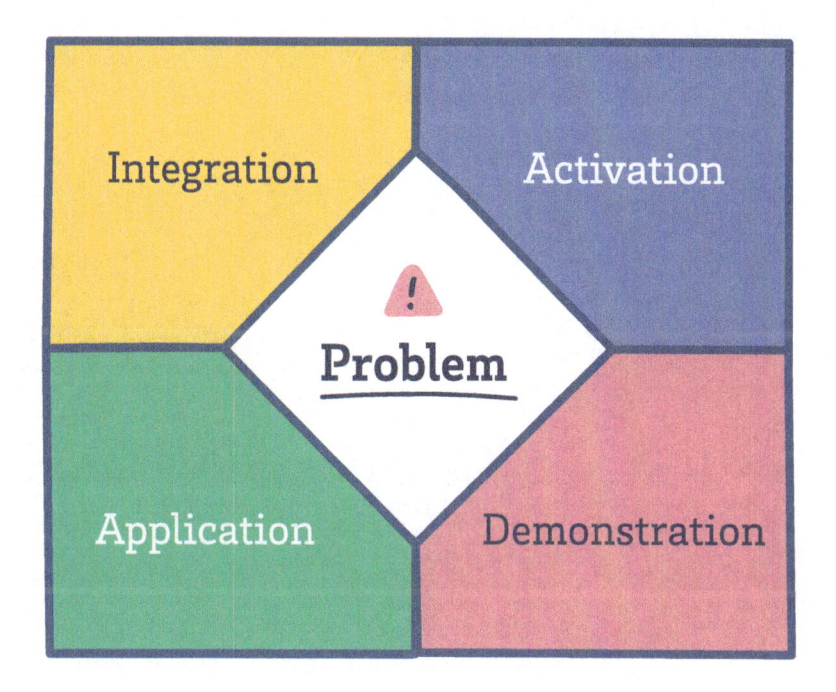

Problem-Centered Information
Activation
Demonstration
Application
Integration

In the next chapter, I'll unpack M. David Merrill's first principles of instruction. As you'll see, these five principles represent the core relationships that underlie any successful learning model or method, including the one we'll be using. Taken together, you can think of these concepts as the master formula for designing any course and it's the formula you'll put to use in Part 2 as you design your course blueprint.

CHAPTER 2

Information is Not Instruction

The First Principles of Instruction

AT THIS POINT, YOU MAY STILL HAVE A nagging question in the back of your mind: Can this book really help me design learning for my target audience when there are so many different contexts and topics in the corporate space? Well, here's the beauty of finding a master formula: The formula can be used in whatever context for whatever topic you have in mind. Don't believe me? Let's dig in and I'll show you.

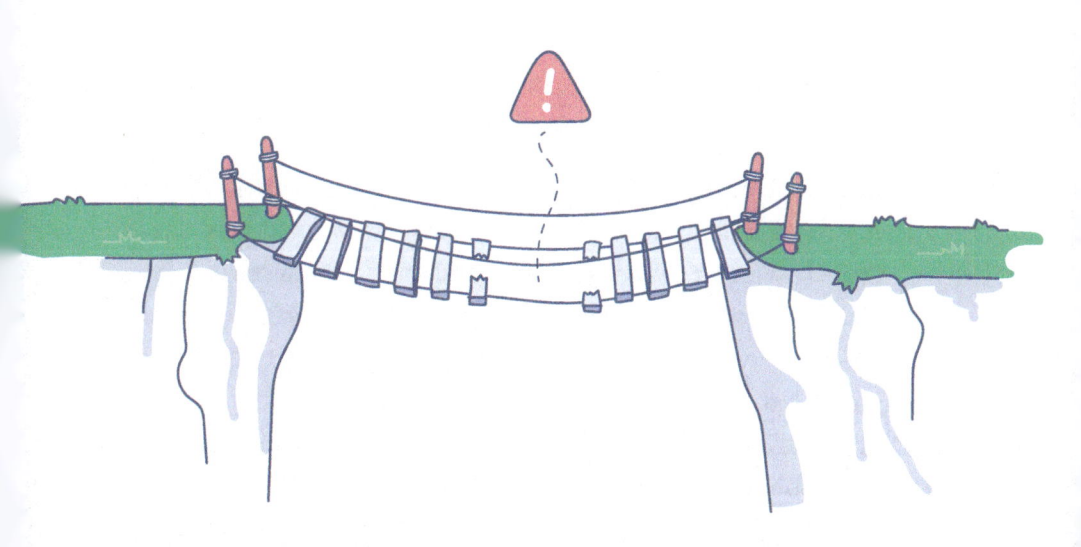

THE PEBBLE-IN-THE-POND MODEL FOR INSTRUCTIONAL DESIGN

After reviewing instructional design theories, models, and research that spans nearly five decades, M. David Merrill identified a set of five interrelated principles. These principles underlie every model or method of instructional design and can be implemented to promote learning activities of all types.

That being said, Merrill prefers what he calls the Pebble-in-the-Pond Model for Instructional Design.[7] Merrill uses the

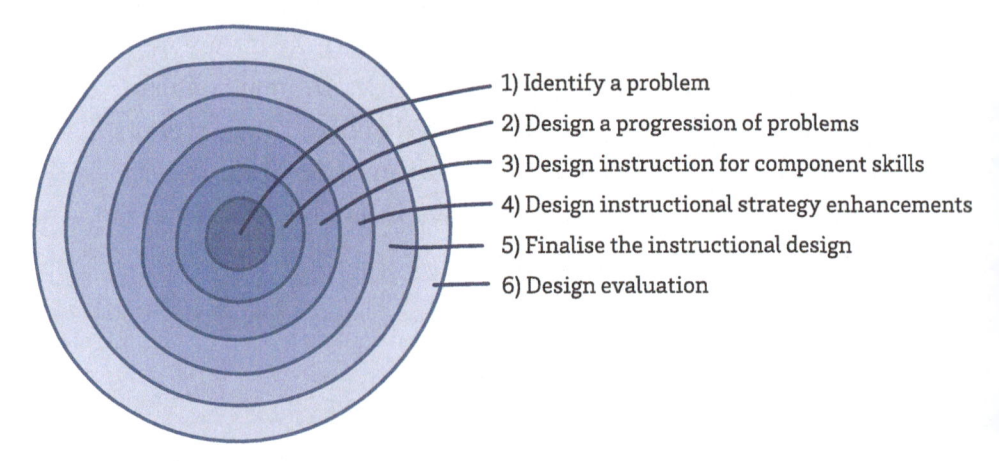

1) Identify a problem
2) Design a progression of problems
3) Design instruction for component skills
4) Design instructional strategy enhancements
5) Finalise the instructional design
6) Design evaluation

metaphor of a pond to illustrate the environment in which instruction is to occur. The pond starts out as smooth as glass. Once you toss a pebble into that pond, though, you see the ripples. The pebble in this case is an instance of a problem learners need to solve. When the "problem pebble" gets tossed into the pond, that is the trigger for the start of the instructional design process. The first ripple consists of a blueprint demonstration and application of this *problem* instance. The second ripple is

---

[7] For an overview of this model, see Chapter 11 of *First Principles of Instruction: Identifying and Designing Effective, Efficient, and Engaging Instruction.*

Information is Not Instruction

a progression of problems of the same type along with demonstrations or applications for each problem in the *progression*. The third ripple is made up of demonstrations or applications for each of the *component skills* required to solve this class of problems. The fourth ripple is *integration and enhancement strategies* added to the demonstrations and applications to improve learning. The fifth ripple is *finalize design*, which includes any visual, navigation, or other supplemental instruction materials you want to add after you complete your course blueprint. The sixth ripple is *evaluation* and includes data collection, feedback, assessment, and blueprint revision.

You will draw from this pebble-in-the-pond metaphor, along with the master formula I introduced earlier and the first principles of instruction, which I discuss next, to design your course blueprint.

In what follows, I filter Merrill's five principles through the lens of my master formula. Fans of M. David Merrill will notice that I present the principles in a different order: problem-centered information, activation, demonstration, application, and integration. I have found this ordering to be more user friendly and better aligned with design thinking.

The 5 First Principles of Instruction:
1. The **activation** principle: Learning is promoted when learners activate relevant prior knowledge or experience.
2. The **task-centered** principle: Learning is promoted when learners engage in a task-centered instructional strategy.
3. The **demonstration** principle: Learning is promoted when learners observe a demonstration.

31

4. The **application** principle: Learning is promoted when learners apply the new knowledge.

5. The **integration** principle: Learning is promoted when learners integrate their new knowledge into their everyday world.

It's not hard to see how these principles describe the essential elements of learning. When students are encouraged to activate prior knowledge for the purpose of completing a task-centered (AKA problem-centered) activity, then observe a demonstration of someone solving the same problem, apply what they learned, and integrate that new knowledge into their world, learning happens.

Now, let's unpack each of these principles so you can begin to see how they might apply to the course you want to create.

Warning: The rest of this chapter gets a bit technical. While you may not totally understand everything now, I promise that once you begin designing your course (soon!), it will become clearer. I've done my best to explain each principle as simply as I can without including a lot of theory. However, if you want to dig deeper into the research behind instructional design, you can check out Chapter 18: Further Research and Resources.

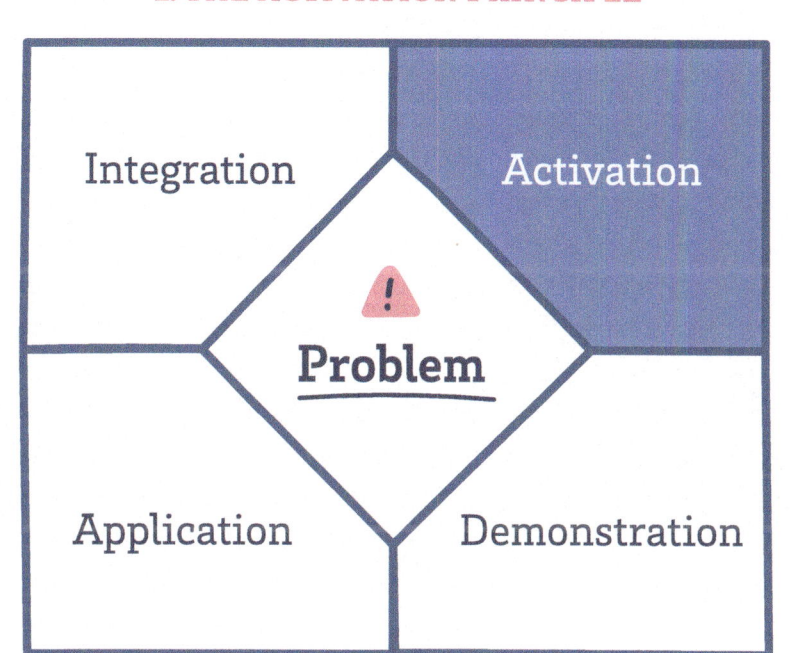

1. THE ACTIVATION PRINCIPLE

```
┌─────────────────┬─────────────────┐
│   Integration   │    Activation   │
│          ╲     ⚠    ╱            │
│           ╲  Problem ╱            │
│           ╱         ╲             │
│   Application  │   Demonstration  │
└─────────────────┴─────────────────┘
```

All learners come to new instruction with a whole suitcase full of prior knowledge. As a highly skilled instructional designer, you can tap into that prior knowledge to increase learning. Activation is the key to unlocking your learners' prior knowledge and experience.

When learners are prompted to activate prior cognitive structures by being instructed to recall, describe, or demonstrate prior knowledge, it enhances their learning. The key here is helping your learners unpack and organize their prior skills into an integrated whole with the new skills you're teaching them. Otherwise, prior knowledge may become baggage weighing down your learners and getting in the way of learning the new skills you're trying to teach. To avoid having to guide your learners through unlearning previous skills, I recommend focusing on activating only prior knowledge that's relevant to the new skills you're teaching.

For example, when you design the final demonstration, make sure the structure you use is similar to what students already know. Not only should you encourage students to relate general information to specific scenarios, you should also ask them to relate old information to the new structure.

Also, throughout the phases of instruction, you can remind students to draw on their previously acquired skills and knowledge in order to help them apply what they have just learned. Whenever you encourage students to summarize what they have learned and examine how the new knowledge relates to what they previously learned within a consistent structure, you set them up for success.

2. THE TASK-CENTERED PRINCIPLE

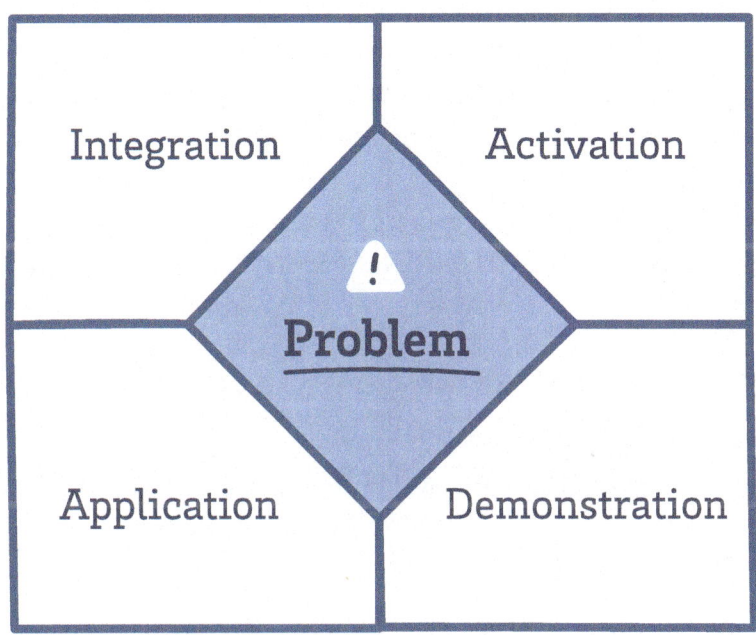

```
Integration        Activation

            ⚠
            Problem

Application        Demonstration
```

Another principle that Merrill observed as underlying all successful instructional design models is the task-centered principle (which you may also understand in relation to a problem-centered model of learning). Basically, learning happens when students tackle a specific task or a series of increasingly complex tasks (I call them problem scenarios) which require them to use all of the skills they've learned.

Merrill sets up the task-centered approach in contrast to other problem-based instructional strategies. One type of problem-based instructional strategy is to give a small group of learners a complex problem to solve, identify resources that can be used to solve the problem, and expect learners to acquire the necessary skills by searching through the resources and

THE DO IT MESSY APPROACH

finding the problem solution through trial and error. In theory, members of the group will learn from each other and cooperate to troubleshoot solutions when they get stuck. However, in practice, this type of open problem solving can be inefficient and ineffective in teaching the desired skills.

Alternatively, the task-centered strategy Merrill discusses gives direct instruction, but in the context of real-world tasks.

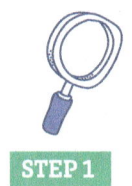

STEP 1   **STEP 2**   **STEP 3**   **STEP 4**   **STEP 5**

Here's how it works:

- Step 1: Identify a task that you want your learners to be able to complete.
- Step 2: Break it down according to the steps, skills, and conditions needed to complete the task.
- Step 3: Create a series of demonstrations (i.e., tell, ask, show, do) designed to teach the relevant steps, skills, and conditions.
- Step 4: Repeat step 3 until you have taught all of the relevant steps, skills, and conditions.
- Step 5: Create a series of applications (i.e., tasks to which learners can apply their skills).

It may be helpful to think of this principle as a series of learning cycles. You might go through this whole process with a relatively simple task. Then you could add on skills and ask learners to apply those new skills, plus the old skills, to complete a more complicated task and so on. As learners develop their skill set, they will be required to do more and more of the task, while the instructional system demonstrates less and less, until they are able to complete the task without any guidance from you.

3. THE DEMONSTRATION PRINCIPLE

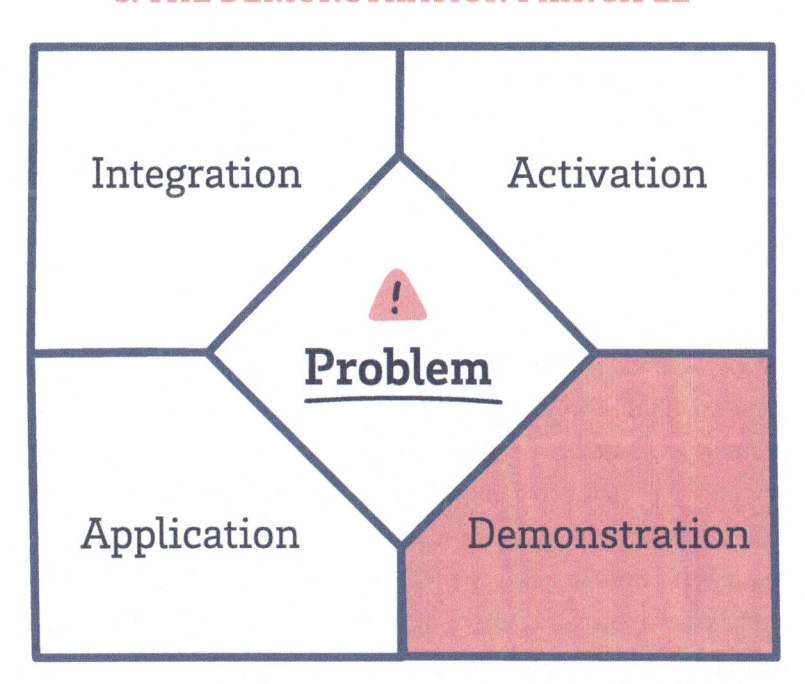

Integration	Activation
⚠️ **Problem**	
Application	**Demonstration**

When learners observe a demonstration (sometimes referred to as a portrayal) of the skills they want to learn and that demonstration is consistent with the type of content they want to learn, this is the first step to success. Demonstration is most helpful when students are guided to consider how the general information being presented relates to specific real-world scenarios.

THE DO IT MESSY APPROACH

Demonstration works best for three types of generalizable skills:

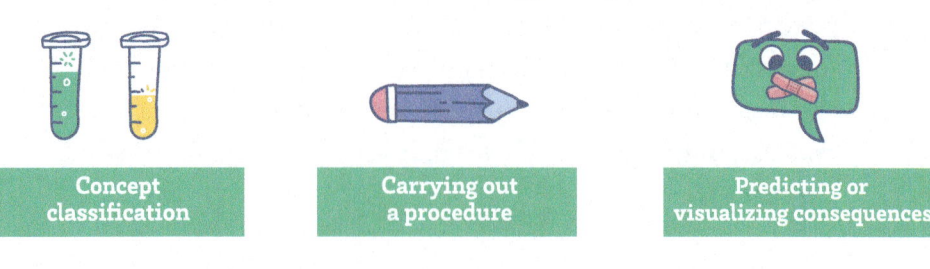

Concept classification | **Carrying out a procedure** | **Predicting or visualizing consequences**

- Concept classification (kinds of): e.g., different types of lab equipment, when to use this chemical vs. that chemical.
- Carrying out a procedure (how-to): e.g., how to write a sales pitch, how to create a template in PowerPoint.
- Predicting or visualizing consequences (what happens): e.g., following safety protocols, what happens when teams don't communicate.

When designing a demonstration, present several scenarios to show how the general information shared earlier in the course applies to specific situations. For example, suppose you were creating a safety video for a construction site, and you wanted to teach someone what happens when they fail to lockout a piece of equipment. In case you're not familiar, lockout procedures are safety protocols that eliminate the risk of someone turning on a piece of machinery while someone else is in a precarious position.

Information is Not Instruction

Here's the demonstration principle at work:

tell   **ask**   **show**   **do**

1. Tell: Present the conditions under which the equipment should be locked out.
2. Ask: Ask the learner to recall the conditions under which equipment should be locked out.
3. Show: Demonstrate the process in several different scenarios.
4. Do: Have the learner apply the conditions to predict the consequences in new lockout scenarios.

> **TIP**
>
> One common mistake instructional designers make is failing to provide sufficient demonstrations. I recommend including three demonstrations (that include all four principles), at a minimum, in your course to promote effective, efficient, and engaging learning.

4. THE APPLICATION PRINCIPLE

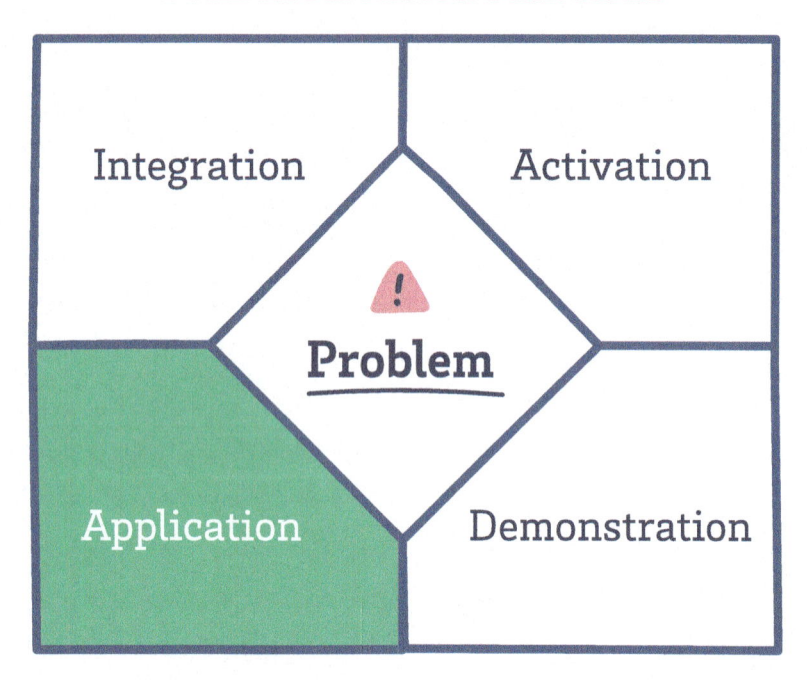

Integration	Activation
	Problem
Application	Demonstration

To apply knowledge is to use the information and skills the learner is in the process of acquiring through demonstrations. Because we are using this instructional design method to teach generalizable knowledge, application happens when learners use the knowledge gained to solve a new problem or complete a different task from the one used in the demonstration.

- Application for concept classification (kinds of) occurs when learners must classify new examples of each category by labeling, sorting, or ranking the examples.
- Application for carrying out a procedure (how-to) occurs when learners are required to carry out each step in a task during a new simulated situation.

- Application for predicting consequences (what happens) occurs when learners are required to predict outcomes from a set of given conditions in a new specific scenario.

When learners apply newly acquired knowledge, this helps them to solidify the skills they have been told about, asked to recall, and shown by observing the demonstrations. But application only results in effective learning when learners receive feedback. Think back to the construction safety video example above. After having the learner predict the consequences, you could have the scenario play out so that the learner can see if the consequences are consistent with their prediction. This would be a form of feedback in this case.

Bonus points: If you want to take this principle a step further, increase the difficulty of application. You can enhance learning for each of the three types of generalizable knowledge in the following ways:

Concept classification **Carrying out a procedure** **Predicting or visualizing consequences**

- For concept classification (kinds of), you could have learners explain their classification.
- For carrying out a procedure (how-to), you could require learners to carry out a progression of increasingly complex tasks and stack skills by making the more complex tasks rely on recalling simpler skills that they have mastered.

- For predicting consequences (what happens), you could require learners to make predictions for an increasingly complex progression of specific scenarios.

5. THE INTEGRATION PRINCIPLE

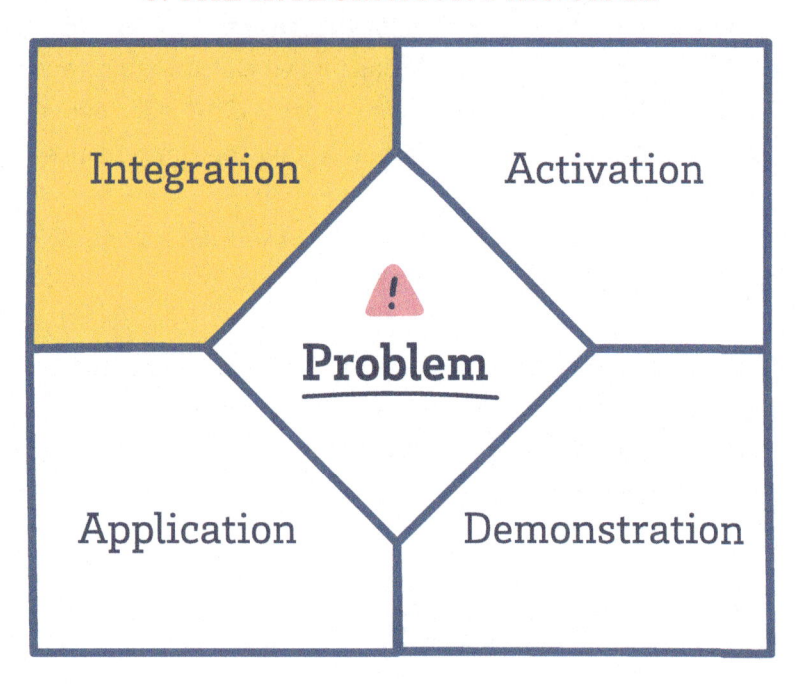

Finally, if you want students to recall and use the information you have provided them in your course (and this should always be the goal when we're adhering to the fundamental laws of instructional design), you need to consider how to help them integrate the knowledge into their everyday lives.

To understand the critical importance of the integration principle, all you need to do is ask yourself what you remember from the foreign language courses you took in school. If you

Information is Not Instruction

took a semester or two of Spanish 101 in college 20 years ago, but haven't spoken Spanish since — except maybe on the odd trip to Cabo — you probably don't remember much. However, if you took four years of Spanish, spent a semester abroad in Spain, and landed a job that required you to communicate with direct reports in Spanish on a daily basis, you're probably pretty skilled at speaking Spanish.

So why do many instructional designers ignore integration? Well, one reason is that it's difficult to put your learners in the role of the teacher. But this is exactly what you need to do to help your learners integrate their skills. When learners have meaningful discussions with others and are put in the position of needing to defend their skills, then they engage in the kind of deep reflection needed to "refine their mental models, eliminate misconceptions, and increase the flexibility with which they use their new skill," says Merrill. Such an opportunity "increases the probability that the skill will be retained and used in the everyday lives of the learners," he continues.[8]

The Integration Principle draws on memory theory.[9] There are two types of memory: explicit and implicit. When we're asked to memorize something or given information that's "for memory's sake only," we're likely to forget large amounts of information quickly, at least without a significant amount of rehearsal. That's because such information gets stored in explicit memory. However, when we develop integrated skills

---

8 Chapter 3 of *First Principles of Instruction: Identifying and Designing Effective, Efficient, and Engaging Instruction.*

9 McClelland, James L., et al. (2020). "Integration of New Information in Memory: New Insights from a Complementary Learning Systems Perspective." *Philosophical Transactions of the Royal Society B: Biological Sciences*, vol. 375, no. 1799. doi:10.1098/rstb.2019.0637.

that we use to complete real-world tasks, the information gets imprinted in implicit memory as a mental model.[10] In this case, we're much less likely to forget and we retain the ability to perform complex tasks over a much longer period. When students learn how to integrate their skills, even after a period of insufficient use, relearning takes much less time.

To effectively integrate the skills you want to teach, consider how you can extend instruction beyond the eLearning or classroom training and into their everyday lives. Keep in mind that humans are natural-born learners. When we perceive that we've acquired a real skill, we're eager and excited to demonstrate it for others. So your integration strategies need not be complicated. Simply suggesting learners share what they have learned may be all the incentive they need.

CONCLUSION

Always being one to practice what I preach, I'm not asking you to memorize these principles. Instead, in the second part of this book, I'll show you exactly how to put these principles into action as you design your course blueprint. But before we get there, we need to address a couple more pieces of housekeeping. Next, I'll walk you through your quick and dirty needs analysis, and I'll help you think through the most strategic way to use subject matter experts (SMEs) as you think about and map out your course.

---

10 Dew ITZ, Cabeza R. (2011). "The Porous Boundaries Between Explicit and Implicit Memory: Behavioral and Neural Evidence." *Annals of the New York Academy of Sciences*. 1224: 174-190. doi:10.1111/j.1749-6632.2010.05946.x

CHAPTER 3

Quick & Dirty

Your Needs Analysis

NOW THAT YOU HAVE SEEN AN OVERVIEW of the five principles of instruction, you are ready to change gears. Before you start creating your course blueprint, you need to answer one more question: Is there a need for my course? A needs analysis will help you find the answer.

THE DO IT MESSY APPROACH

THINK LIKE A JOURNALIST

If you have never performed a needs analysis before, then you're probably wondering where to start. I tell my students to start by putting on their journalist's hat. Why? Thinking like a journalist strips away all of the distractions and gets straight to the key questions you need to answer. These questions will help you identify the content area, primary learning goal, metrics to watch, and the learner population for instruction.

Journalists famously use the "five W's" to get to the bones of their storytelling. When they feel satisfied that they have complete answers to these questions, they are ready to write their story.

The 5 W's:

- Who?
- What?
- Where?
- When?
- Why?

Similarly, when you answer a series of questions falling into four buckets, you'll be ready to create your course. There are four W's making up the bones of your course:

The 4 W's of your course blueprint design:

- Who are your learners?
- What are the organizational challenges you need to solve?
- What do you want learners to be able to do at the end of instruction?
- What are your constraints?

Answering these questions will give you a solid structure on which to build the rest of your course content. If you don't know who your learners are, then you'll add irrelevant information to your course. Likewise, if you aren't sure what organizational challenges your learners need to overcome, your course will miss the mark. And so on. These are important questions to answer before you begin creating content — at least if you want to be efficient, effective, and engaging.

THE DO IT MESSY APPROACH

THE PITFALLS OF NEEDS ANALYSIS

If you *have* performed a needs analysis before, then it's likely that you're picturing a complex process full of data collection and red tape. Allow me to disabuse you of this notion now. I want to demystify the needs analysis process for you in this chapter, and that's why we're narrowing our focus to the four buckets mentioned above.

Before we examine each of the four W's and related questions, however, we need to get familiar with some of the pitfalls of needs analysis. One of the pitfalls is overthinking, and it trips up a lot of IDOLs. Because it's so easy to overthink your needs analysis, it's important that you carefully follow what I've laid out here and ignore the temptation to fall down any rabbit holes. My needs analysis process is intentionally quick and dirty because thorough analysis is more likely to produce paralysis than a course blueprint. If you're not careful, however, you'll end up trying to refine your course before you've built the blueprint, and this is the fastest way to never having a course you feel ready to share with the world.

Also, if you believe you need to do a full audience analysis when the organization already has a lot of great material to share with you about their audience, take a step back and consider whether you really need to reinvent the wheel. Make sure to take advantage of all the institutional knowledge available and how much you know already. The data they have to share might not be perfect, but it could be all that you need to get started.

Finally, needs shift over time. That's just a fact of life. If you spend months on your needs analysis, it's very likely that the

Quick & Dirty

> 💡 **TIP**
>
> In addition to overthinking, I've seen instructional designers fall into three more needs analysis pitfalls: overcomplicating the needs analysis process, underestimating how much they already know, and forgetting that needs shift over time. You might be tempted to overcomplicate the process by interviewing 100 employees, for example. I recommend that you interview no more than five people before building your blueprint. And ideally, your interview pool should be diverse, so you get a variety of perspectives. Consider interviewing employees (including a mix of high performers and underperformers, usually identified by the business stakeholders or supervisors) and supervisors. The goal of these preliminary interviews is to help you create your learner personas or avatars, so you know how to tailor your course to meet their needs. Interviewing more than five people, however, will likely give you too much conflicting data that will take a lot of time to sort through and distract you from the core of what you need to teach. Remember, you can only do so much within one course. Use these preliminary interviews to narrow down your learners' needs.

organization's needs will change during that time. Instead, opt to get down to business quickly and solve an immediate problem. I recommend you spend no more than a week or two on your needs analysis. This way, you prove that you can adapt with the organization and you'll be more likely to be tapped to create the next training solution or course.

Does all of this sound too simple? Okay then, I want you to think about the Wright Brothers for a moment. What would have happened if they had spent years doing a lengthy needs analysis — interviewing every Tom, Dick, and Harry they met in the street, tracking down every expert in wind speed, throwing out everything they knew about bicycle mechanics because after all, they were building a flying contraption, and trying to solve every problem they could come up with? Well, it's very likely that someone else would have been the first in flight and no one would know the names Orville and Wilbur Wright outside of Dayton, Ohio. I hope this is enough to convince you to try your needs analysis my way.

The quick and dirty needs analysis process I lay out next is designed to help you avoid these pitfalls and more.

22 QUESTIONS: YOUR QUICK & DIRTY NEEDS ANALYSIS

Returning to the four W's of course blueprint design, we'll now look at the critical questions to ask within each bucket. Together, answering these 22 questions will serve as your needs analysis. They will give you everything you need to know to get started on your course content. If you get stuck, remember to return to these questions. They are your guiding light on the path to building your blueprint. Also, once you have finished your blueprint, you'll want to do a gut check by returning to these questions and using them as a quick and dirty checklist.

Here are our 4 W's once again:

- Who are your learners?
- What are the organizational challenges you need to solve?
- What do you want learners to be able to do at the end of instruction?
- What are your constraints?

You will want to complete your needs analysis before designing your course blueprint. So grab a pen and a notebook and start answering these 22 questions now. Or go to my resources webpage and grab a digital download with all these questions included here: www.idolcourses.com/doitmessy.

Who are your learners?

First, it's important to get clear on who your learners are. For instance, if you are training a group of subject matter experts, you'll offer different instruction than if you are training a mixed or general audience. The following six questions will help you get a handle on who your learners are.

1. Who are the learners and what are their roles?
    - What is their stake in this? Who is: Responsible, Accountable, Consulted, Informed?
2. What does the target audience look like?
    - How many people? Are they all playing the same or different roles? Are they all roughly equally experienced or are you training new starters? Do they all have access to the technology you need to train them?
    - Is this training mandatory? What are the language requirements? When will they take this training?

THE DO IT MESSY APPROACH

> How much time do they have to take this training? Where would they look for information/support?

3. Do the learners work in offices or engage in physical labor? (This defines how to best deliver the course.)
   - Under what circumstances will they need to use what they learn? What are the common constraints or challenges?
4. What is their experience with this topic?
   - What do they already know? What don't they know? Do they think they need this training? What is the learners' level of urgency to learn this task? Do they have any preconceptions about this topic? What kinds of mistakes are they making and why?
5. Which (5) employees and supervisors can you talk to who experience/are impacted by the problem/challenge?
6. Which other departments or people are affected by this problem/challenge?

What are the organizational challenges you need to solve?

Once you get to know your target learners, it's time to look at the challenge the organization needs you to address. Then you can play the role of matchmaker to figure out how to meet your learners where they are and bridge the gap with your course. It's best to talk directly to the stakeholders, if possible, to get a sense of how they view the challenge your course will solve. You can ask the following five questions to help you understand the organizational challenge.

7. What is the problem/challenge you are trying to address?
8. Do you have an idea for a solution in mind already?
9. Are there existing/immediate issues and/or behaviors that need addressing?
10. What are the risks/challenges we need to consider?
11. Have you done a root cause analysis for the problem/challenge? What is the result?

What do you want learners to be able to do at the end of instruction?

Essentially, this bucket is all about you proving the worth of your course. You can think of these questions as leading to the success conditions or learning outcomes. If you get the organization to sign off on this list, and you deliver on your promise, then your course is golden. Here are the six questions to ask to understand what you want your learners to be able to do after taking your training course.

12. What is the business reason for this request?
13. What areas affect the desired outcome?
    - Knowledge, Capabilities, Motivation, Organizational barriers...
14. What changes will we see in the organization when we implement this solution? What does success look like?
15. What will happen if we do nothing? What is the impact on the organization?
16. How can we measure the impact of the solution (with existing means)?

17. What materials are available already and where can I find them? Are those materials being used?
    - What works, what does not (proven)? What is reusable? What is scalable?

What are your constraints?

Finally, you will need to know what constraints you're working with. Sure, you can promise the moon with an unlimited budget and all the time in the world to deliver, but here on Earth, you need to set expectations based on the limitations you receive. Here are five questions to get at those constraints.

18. Which technical requirements and limitations do we need to take into account?
19. Which means are available for implementation?
20. Is there a known budget (or range)?
21. What is the desired timeline? Why this timeline?
22. Is there anything relevant to this project I should know that I haven't asked about?

With these 22 questions answered, your needs analysis is complete and you are almost ready to move on to Part 2: Blueprint Design. Yes, really! You may find through trial and error that you need to ask a few more questions, tailored to your course material and your particular audience of learners. And that's okay. But this gives you a good starting point. And I can't emphasize enough how important it is to avoid *paralysis by analysis* in the beginning. So no overthinking!

For further thoughts and readings about your needs analysis, check out Chapter 18: Further Research and Resources.

CHAPTER 4

It's Pronounced "Smee"

Subject Matter Experts

RECALL THAT THE FORMULA I'M teaching here for creating your course blueprint hinges on a task-centered or problem-based approach. In other words, you will measure the success of your course

THE DO IT MESSY APPROACH

according to how well your learners can complete a specific task or solve one problem. So how do you ensure that your learners succeed? You provide them with real-world demonstrations and applications.

In this chapter, I reveal the secret to creating task-centered or problem-based activities with real-world implications: Interview subject matter experts (SMEs).

There are four ways to gain access to SMEs:

1. Work on a project with a paying client (part-time, full-time, or contract),
2. Work with a volunteer client,
3. Interview a knowledgeable colleague or friend, or
4. Be your own SME and simply make up scenarios based on your own knowledge and experience.

In all four cases, there is a SME whose experience you can draw upon to craft scenarios for your learners. If you have a current paying client who is dealing with a challenge that your course blueprint promises to address, all you have to do is ask if you can shadow them or interview them about how they complete a particular task to gather ideas for scenarios you can script out. Also, because your course promises to solve a current challenge for them, they are likely to be open to helping you out.

What if you don't have any paying clients yet? You can find volunteer clients by contacting local nonprofits, online organizations, friends who own small businesses, the local library, or by posting in a relevant Facebook group (or on your preferred social media platform).

Here's a simple template you can use to reach out to potential SMEs:

> Hi! I'm [your name here] and I create online learning content for adults. I love your organization because of [specific reason you love them]. I am currently looking to expand my skills and portfolio. I want to build my portfolio based on real problems for a real purpose. Therefore, I am offering to create training for your organization for free in exchange for permission to use samples in my portfolio. I'd be happy to chat more about your needs and my process. Schedule a time with me here [insert calendar link].

Alternatively, you could look at a particular project you're working on with a group of colleagues and ask one of them to demonstrate how they complete a particular task. And if you don't have direct access to SMEs through the work you do, you can create a portfolio of different scenarios by interviewing a friend or colleague, or tap into your own subject matter expertise by making up some scenarios based on situations you have observed.

TIPS FOR GETTING QUALITY FEEDBACK FROM SMES

After you have identified your SMEs, talked with them about their needs, and created your course blueprint with all of this in mind, you'll return to them to get feedback on what you've shared. Even if you're brand new to instructional design, it's important to approach SMEs with confidence. Knowing what feedback will be most helpful for you and directing your SMEs to give you the information you need is key to getting this right.

Here are a few tips about getting quality feedback from SMEs:

- **Ask specific questions tailored to your course:** Instead of simply sharing your course and asking, "what do you think?," you should come up with a list of specific questions that will help you improve your course. Ask questions like: What did you enjoy most about this course? What did you enjoy the least? Where were you confused? Did you notice any gaps in information?
- **Be open to the feedback you receive:** Receiving feedback can be hard on the ego. Keep in mind that your SMEs want to help and any criticism is an opportunity for you to become better at instructional design. This will help you be more open to receiving other perspectives. Listen to the feedback begin given, consider it honestly, and then decide whether to incorporate it.
- **Understand the message:** Check to make sure you understand the feedback you're getting. Ask clarifying questions as needed. Repeat what you're hearing to ensure you're interpreting the feedback correctly.
- **Follow up:** This could mean simply implementing the feedback you're given, setting up another meeting to discuss the feedback, or sharing the updated version of your course and asking for additional feedback on the revisions.

Throughout this process, do your best to keep your emotions in check. If you have a SME who doesn't follow, it can feel as if you're taking orders. Always remember that this is your course. At the end of the day, SMEs are a resource for you. You are free to reflect and decide how to incorporate (or not) whatever feedback you receive. If you disagree with someone's feedback, you may want to seek another opinion.

CAPTURE ALL OF THE STEPS

Perhaps the biggest challenge in teaching anyone how to do anything is making sure that you do not leave out any steps. Skipping a crucial step in one of your demonstrations will leave your learner confused and unable to apply the skills you're trying to teach them. This is precisely why I recommend shadowing or interviewing subject matter experts as opposed to simply jumping into scripting your course. If you skip this step, you're more likely to miss something critical.

Again, recall the breakdown of the task-centered strategy for creating your course blueprint:

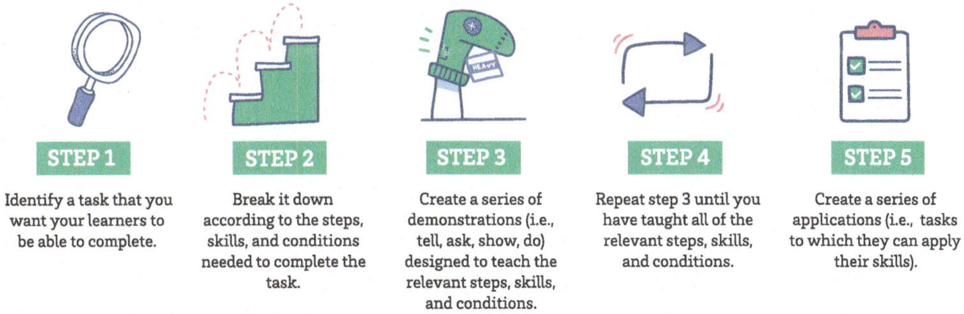

STEP 1 — Identify a task that you want your learners to be able to complete.

STEP 2 — Break it down according to the steps, skills, and conditions needed to complete the task.

STEP 3 — Create a series of demonstrations (i.e., tell, ask, show, do) designed to teach the relevant steps, skills, and conditions.

STEP 4 — Repeat step 3 until you have taught all of the relevant steps, skills, and conditions.

STEP 5 — Create a series of applications (i.e., tasks to which they can apply their skills).

- Step 1: Identify a task that you want your learners to be able to complete.
- Step 2: Break it down according to the steps, skills, and conditions needed to complete the task.
- Step 3: Create a series of demonstrations (i.e., tell, ask, show, do) designed to teach the relevant steps, skills, and conditions.
- Step 4: Repeat Step 3 until you have taught all of the relevant steps, skills, and conditions.
- Step 5: Create a series of applications (i.e., tasks to which they can apply their skills).

SMEs can help you out, especially with Steps 1 and 2. Suppose you need to teach a group of customer service providers the ins and outs of a software application, like MailChimp, so that they can offer customer support. After you complete your quick and dirty needs analysis, a great next step would be to find a software superuser to serve as your SME — again, this could be a client, a colleague, or a friend — and ask them to show you how they use the software. If you happen to be a superuser and want to serve as your own SME, a good strategy is to record yourself using the software. Either way, this technique will give you clues into the types of subtasks your students will need to complete, as well as the steps, skills, and conditions needed to complete the main task (in other words, this is the start of your task analysis). While your SME does the demonstration for you, take note of the required skills and start brainstorming the series of demonstrations needed to achieve your course learning outcomes.

Using SMEs in this way, you can quickly design the whole problem (AKA the Whole Shebang) or complex task set and start brainstorming your problem scenarios based on real world examples. You can use the stories your SMEs share and ask direct questions to gather a lot of great material for your course design.

A NOTE ON USING YOURSELF AS A SUBJECT MATTER EXPERT

Using yourself as the subject matter expert (SME) is not a bad idea, especially if you are the number one expert at your organization or in your field. But, you need to remember that as an expert, you are different from the novices you will be teaching.

TIP

To overcome this challenge, write down all of the steps you can think of needed to solve your task, then record yourself following the steps. Do your best to stop yourself from unconsciously filling in any gaps. Instead, strictly follow the steps as you have written them. It may be helpful to imagine teaching an alien how to make a peanut butter and jelly sandwich or giving a stranger instructions to sketch an image while they're wearing a blindfold. This should help unmask any gaps in your protocol. Or better yet, test out your steps on a novice to see if they can complete the task.

Another tip here is to treat the tasks you're demonstrating as if you were creating Standard Operating Procedures (SOPs) for a protégé. Imagine you have to explain how to solve this problem to someone in the third grade. I know it may feel like you're dumbing down the material, but remember, you're a SME and you're not likely creating a course for other SMEs. If your demonstration becomes too elementary, you can always take out steps later — while providing links to earlier lessons or resources for those who need extra help. It's best to be as explicit as possible, at least at the beginning.

THE DO IT MESSY APPROACH

As an expert, you have acquired knowledge that affects what you notice as well as how you organize, represent, and interpret information. The paradox is that the more you know, the more blind you become to what your learners don't know.[11] This means that you may inadvertently skip steps that your learners need to see spelled out.

Finally, as you're identifying tasks that you want your learners to be able to complete, keep in mind that you may want to divide the tasks into main tasks and subtasks. I'll talk much more about how to define tasks in Part 2, but to help you picture how this might work, here is an example of a task analysis (note that this is different from the needs analysis I discussed in chapter 3) for a nightly skincare routine.

TASK ANALYSIS:

The Whole Shebang or Big Problem: How to complete a full, nightly skincare routine.

Main Tasks:

Daily tasks:

1. Wipe off makeup (if you're wearing makeup)
2. Wash face with a cleanser
3. Tone skin with a toner
4. Apply an essence
5. Apply a serum

---

[11] See the Dunning-Kruger Effect: https://thedecisionlab.com/biases/dunning-kruger-effect

6. Apply an eye cream
7. Apply a moisturizing lotion

2-3 times a week tasks:

1. Exfoliate face
2. Apply a sheet mask

Main and Subtasks:

1. Wipe off Makeup (if you're wearing makeup)
    a. Use a makeup wipe or micellar water with a cotton pad to wipe off eye and face makeup. This can also be done with an oil cleanser.
    b. Once the wipe or cotton pad has removed all the makeup, move to the next step.
2. Wash Face with a cleanser
    a. Turn on the water.
    b. Wet the entire face and neck.
    c. Dispense about a dime-size amount of product into your hand.
    d. Apply the product to the entire face in small circular motions.
    e. Rinse all the product off of the face.
    f. Dry face with a clean washcloth or let it air dry.
3. Tone skin with a toner
    a. Using hands or a cotton pad, dispense toner.
    b. Apply toner to the entire face and neck.
    c. Wait for the toner to dry.

THE DO IT MESSY APPROACH

4. Apply an Essence
    a. Mist face with the essence or apply with a cotton pad.
5. Apply a serum
    a. Add 3 drops of serum into your hand.
    b. Apply serum all over the face and neck.
    c. Wait for the product to dry.
6. Apply an eye cream
    a. Squeeze a small amount of eye cream onto your ring finger.
    b. Lightly pat the cream underneath and around the eyes.
7. Apply a moisturizing lotion
    a. Dispense a quarter-size amount of moisturizer into your hand.
    b. Gently massage the lotion into the face and neck.
    c. Let it dry.

Were you to interview a SME here, you would watch them demonstrate — or even better — have them record themselves demonstrating each of the main and subtasks you have ideally identified ahead of time. This will give you a window into exactly what you need to teach. The steps and skills are all there. All you have to do now is map out what skills you will be teaching and come up with your scripts.

Combine these SME demonstrations with your quick and dirty needs analysis and you are well on your way to becoming an IDOL. Speaking of which, now it's your turn!

It's Pronounced "Smee"

STOP HERE and do an initial task analysis for your course. Go back to the course topic or business challenge you identified earlier and make a list of all the related main tasks and subtasks. If you need help coming up with a comprehensive list, connect with your SMEs and ask to shadow them during a demonstration. This will help you identify the tasks, steps, skills, and conditions you should cover in your course.

In Part 2, I will walk you through the steps you need to create your own course blueprint using your task analysis. Again, each lesson in Part 2 is designed to help you build each piece of your blueprint in about 20 minutes. You can move through the following lessons as quickly or as slowly as you want, however, finishing your course blueprint in less than 30 days or working in small chunks over the next several months.

Regardless of the pace you choose, the best way to use this next part of the book is to read along and DO. The exercises are designed to build on one another. So rather than reading this book cover to cover, dive in and start creating. If you get stuck, take a break and then get back to work. Remember, the essence of the Do It Messy Approach is for you to focus on what matters most to your learners – what they need to be able to solve the problem (AKA the Whole Shebang) your course teaches them how to solve. Try to avoid getting bogged down in details that don't matter.

Once you have completed your course blueprint, you can turn your attention to design elements and refining your course. Your goal for now is to create a blueprint, not a perfect course (which, by the way, doesn't exist). Get in there and do it messy!

A Note on Tech Tools

One lingering question you might have at the outset is which technology tools to use. I don't have a list of specific tech tools I recommend to my students in the IDOL courses Academy^{SM}, nor do I recommend that you spend a lot of time researching or debating which tools to use. If you've created an online course before and know how to use a certain set of tools, then go ahead and use those for this course as well. Otherwise, you may want to spend about 30 minutes – yes, only 30 minutes – reading up on the different options available (check out the Course Development Tools List included in Chapter 18) before making a decision. It's easy to fall down the rabbit hole looking into tech tools, and while I love a good research rabbit hole as much as the next instructional designer, this won't help you get your course blueprint done. So do yourself a favor and create your messy course before you lose yourself in the search for the perfect tech tools.

> **TIP**
>
> And I will offer one further piece of advice here: If you have never used eLearning tools to design a course or online training, learn one type of tool at a time. For example, if you've never edited video before, start with whatever video editing software you have easy access to (e.g., iMovie, if you're a Mac user) and learn how to use it, before moving on to the next type of tool you need.

Also, keep in mind that designing the content of your course is more important than playing around with various tools that you may or may not end up using. The next several chapters walk you through a step-by-step process to create your course content. You can literally do all the work in a simple Word or Google document and worry about the tech – creating your slides, building your animations, recording your video, editing your video, etc. – later. This is exactly the process I teach my IDOLs, by the way.

Design like a superhero! This is exactly what the Do it Messy Approach teaches. To get to a complete course blueprint, you must forget about the tech and all of the other "what-if's." Forget about your own development skills and design your course as if you can hire people to make the vision come to life based on your blueprint. All you have to do is dive in and get started.

Messy and finished is better than flawless but incomplete. Your skills will grow ten times faster if you design 20 new course blueprints, rather than spending a year trying to make one perfect course.

Let's go!

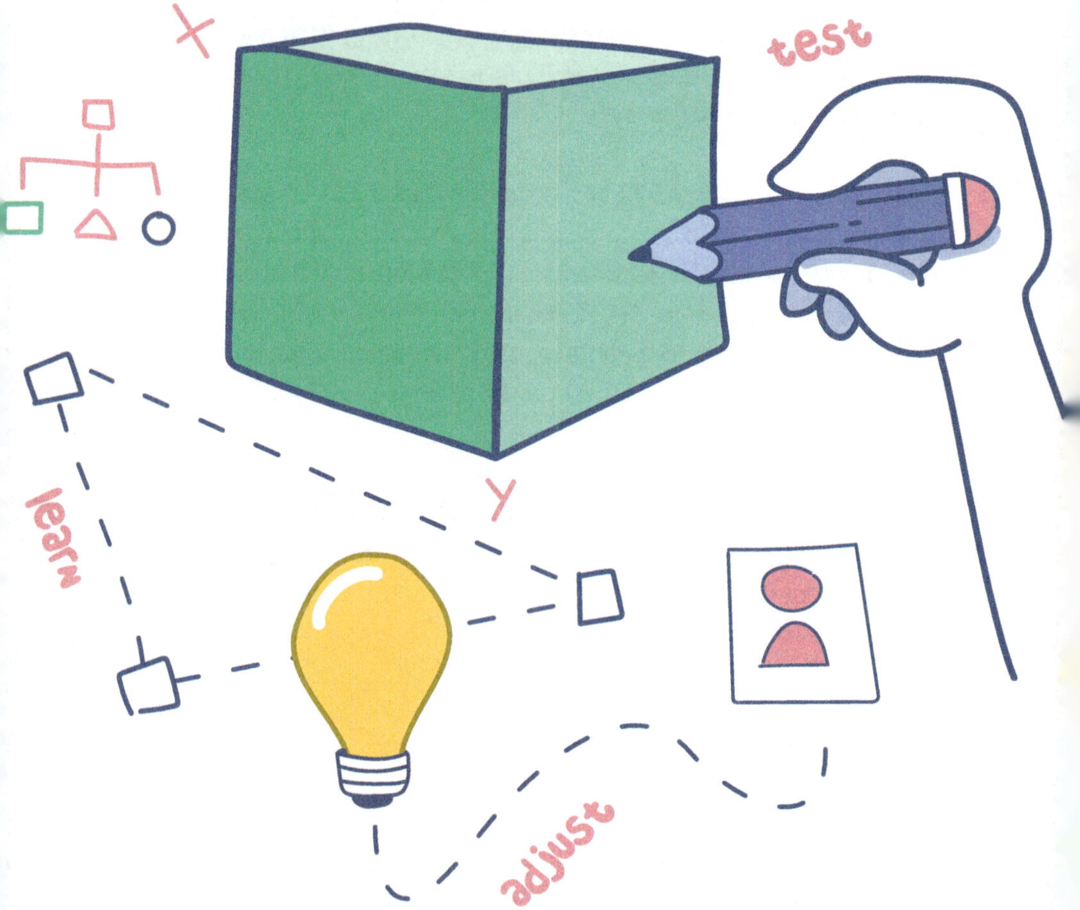
test
learn
adjust

PART TWO

REVERSE ENGINEERING YOUR BLUEPRINT DESIGN

CHAPTER 5

Well, There's Your Problem

Identify a Problem

WITH ALL OF THE PRELIMINARY prep work out of the way, you're ready to start creating your course blueprint. Are you excited? I'm excited for you!

Before you dive into the work of identifying the problem your course will help learners solve, I want to remind you to take action as you read. It's time for the rubber to meet the road, which means if you have been putting off choosing a course topic, you need to put your procrastinating ways behind you.

THE DO IT MESSY APPROACH

It may be helpful at this point to return to the Introduction and re-read the section labeled, "What's your course topic or business challenge?" Take a few minutes now to brainstorm. You will also find checklists at the end of each chapter. These are to help you stay on track, so don't skip over them.

YOUR FIRST JOB: IDENTIFY THE WHOLE PROBLEM (AKA THE WHOLE SHEBANG)

Recall that the foundation of your course blueprint is scripting out task-centered scenarios for your learners to solve. This task-centered or problem-centered approach allows learners to draw on previous knowledge, engage in real world problem solving, apply what they learn immediately and repeatedly, and integrate their newfound knowledge into their worlds.

In other words, we're following M. David Merrill's five first principles of instruction:

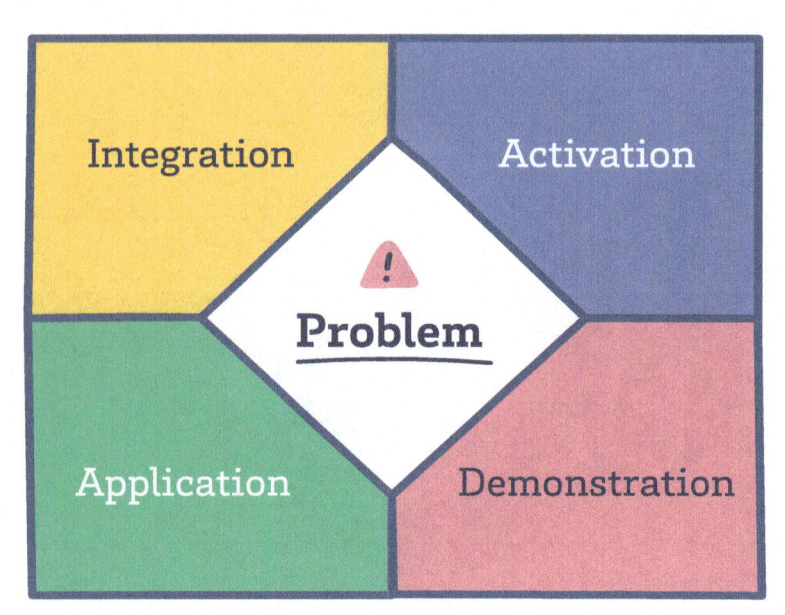

The 5 First Principles of Instruction:

1. The **activation** principle: Learning is promoted when learners activate relevant prior knowledge or experience.
2. The **task-centered** principle: Learning is promoted when learners engage in a task-centered instructional strategy.
3. The **demonstration** principle: Learning is promoted when learners observe a demonstration.
4. The **application** principle: Learning is promoted when learners apply the new knowledge.
5. The **integration** principle: Learning is promoted when learners integrate their new knowledge into their everyday world.

So it makes sense that your first job when it comes to building your course blueprint is to identify the big problem you want your learners to solve. You can quickly find the problem by asking yourself, what is the "problem pebble" that has triggered the start of the instructional design process?

Once you know what problem is under the microscope, you can build the course by revisiting your task analysis and designing a progression of problem scenarios.

The statement of the Whole Shebang will include the information that you're giving the learner in your course and the transformation that will result when the learner has solved the problem. After you identify the big problem, you will design several demonstrations showing the steps needed to solve it and several application exercises that require learners to solve the problem on their own with or without guidance.[12]

THE CHALLENGES WITH IDENTIFYING A PROBLEM

Because you have already completed your needs analysis in Chapter 3 (if you haven't done this yet, STOP, go back, and do it before you continue reading), you should feel ready to identify the big problem you want your learners to solve. Choosing an appropriate problem may seem easy at first, but as you begin to build out your course, you may find yourself rethinking the problem you want to solve. In fact, you may discover that creating your course *is just* a series of iterations on presenting the problem and showing your learners how to solve it from different angles. To save some time, the first thing to consider is what obstacles could get in the way of identifying an appropriate problem or class of problems for your course.

Just like Goldilocks, you need to identify a problem that is "just right." If the problem is too big, you may need to break it down into several courses or modules. If the problem is too small, you risk wasting your learners' time by asking them to solve problems they already understand well.

You also should consider the length of the course you're aiming to create. With brand new instructional designers, for instance, I recommend creating several portfolio assets that you can share with potential clients. Often, these portfolio pieces are created for free for volunteer clients (I mentioned

---

[12] M. David Merrill's *First Principles of Instruction: Identifying and Designing Effective, Efficient, and Engaging Instruction*, (2013), p. 254.

using volunteer clients as SMEs in Chapter 4). Because these are not paid projects, I encourage new IDOLs to set clear boundaries. I tell them to start by creating 30-minute mini-courses and to spend no more than three weeks working on a portfolio course for a volunteer client. The big problem for a mini-course will look very different from the big problem for a mega-course with several different modules.

Now, let's look at how to identify a problem. Suppose you have been hired as an independent contractor by Green Possum, Inc., a manufacturer of environmentally friendly cleaning products. Green Possum has strong direct-to-consumer sales through their eCommerce channels. Now, they're looking to expand operations by getting their products into big box retailers and local grocery chains nationwide.

To accomplish this, Green Possum is expanding its sales team to support the move into wholesale, and you need to design training on the entire product line for all of the new hires. There's only one problem: The new sales team doesn't have much experience pitching wholesale reps. Your job is to train them in how to pitch wholesalers representing big box retailers and local grocery chains.

Your course topic is set, but what is the big problem your course needs to address?
To answer this question, we'll tackle the scenario step-by-step below. Before we get into those details, though, let's look at a couple of problems your course doesn't need to address.

Clearly, if you were to try to train your learners on ALL the different sales techniques they could possibly apply, you would likely leave them feeling confused and ineffective. This problem is too big to tackle in a single course. Also, because you want your course to be as practical as possible, it's best to focus on a problem that lends itself to different scenarios your learners are likely to encounter. Focusing on several different sales processes or techniques doesn't sound very practical.

On the other end of the spectrum, were you to train them on using one sales approach to pitch each and every product in the Green Possum line individually, you would likely find yourself repeating a lot of the same information and asking your trainees to go over information that they already know.

Instead, you want to find a problem that is practical and realistically solvable within the single course you are designing. To get to your big problem, you need to consider the performance goal.

STATE THE PERFORMANCE GOAL

First, you need to clearly understand the performance goal or learning outcome you are aiming for. The outcome should include measurable objectives written with the ABCD formula in mind:[13]

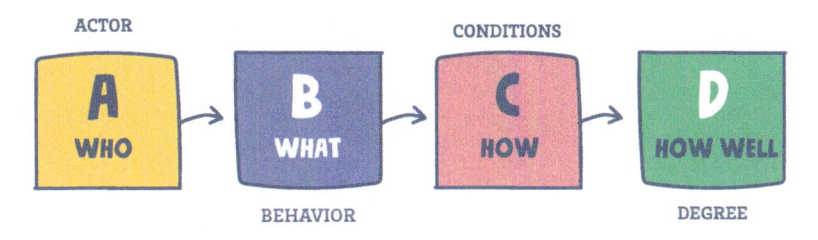

```
ACTOR              CONDITIONS
  A  →   B   →   C   →   D
 WHO    WHAT     HOW    HOW WELL
       BEHAVIOR         DEGREE
```

- Audience: Who will achieve the objective?
- Behavior: What observable behavior shows mastery of the objective?
- Condition: Under what conditions should they be able to perform the behavior?
- Degree: Are there additional criteria for acceptable performance (e.g., speed, accuracy, quality)?

Ideally, you will have a hand in shaping the performance goal as well as getting it approved by your client or organization ahead of time. When you know the goal, you can then decide which class of problems will lead your learners in accomplishing that goal.

Here are some examples of possible performance goals based on the Green Possum, Inc. example:
- We want our sales team to create a pitch script for each main product line and role play with each other weekly based on their real-world experiences.
- We want our sales team to increase sales to big box retailers by 10% next quarter.

---

13 Mager, R. F. (1962). *Preparing Instructional Objectives*. Palo Alto, Calif.: Fearon Publishers.

- We want our sales team to increase their close rate by 50% by the end of the year.
- We want our sales team to get at least one product line into every big box store within a 25-mile radius.

IDENTIFYING YOUR PROBLEM

Once you're clear on the performance goal, it's time to identify a problem that, when solved, will accomplish the performance goal. Specify a problem that includes the information that the learner already brings to the task and the transformation that will result when the problem is solved.

The best way to accomplish this is to design a demonstration of the problem that shows in detail every step required to solve the problem, which is what you'll be working on in the next chapter. Think of your course as the bridge between where your learners are now and where you want them to be in the end.

Here are some examples of problems corresponding to the above learning goals:
- How to deliver a sales pitch to big box retailers
- How to increase sales to big box retailers
- How to increase your sales close rate
- How to get wholesale reps to say "yes" to a product demonstration

Well, There's Your Problem

Here is an example of a script demonstrating how to set up the whole problem:

Slide 1: Title/Intro
Text Title: How to deliver a sales pitch to big box retailers
Slide 2: Setting the Scene
Text Text box 1: Congratulations! You just landed a new sales position. You've been hired to sell Green Possum, Inc. products to wholesale reps at big box stores. Text box 2: Although you have sales experience, you're a little nervous because you've never pitched big box wholesalers. Text box 3: You know your sales target as a team is to increase sales by 10% this year and you want to do your part to help meet that goal. But there's a lot to learn and you're not sure where to start. Text box 4: What's a new salesperson to do?
Slide 3: Introducing the Whole Shebang
Text Text box 1: Luckily, you have Nicole! Text box 2: Nicole has been the manager of sales at Green Possum, Inc. for five years. You (and everyone else) admire her sales record. If anyone can close a sale, she can. Text box 3: Nicole has agreed to mentor you as you practice your pitch and learn the ropes in your new sales role. Text box 4: If you need help during this training, click on Nicole's icon. She'll have some advice for you.

Slide 4: Activation and Steps Needed to Solve the Whole Shebang

Text

A sales pitch is a condensed version of a sales presentation. Ideally, in less than two minutes, you will explain how Green Possum, Inc.'s green cleaning products work, how they solve your rep's pain points, and the benefits they bring to big box customers. Your pitch should end with an invitation to a longer conversation where you can respond to objections and discuss more details.

Before you get started, click on the icons to learn Nicole's approach to pitching big box stores.

Icon 1: **Step 1: How to start your pitch.** Starting a pitch is the hardest part. You have to hook your prospect, so they will actually hear the value of the product and how it will benefit their business. When starting your pitch, you will want to integrate the following: start with the problem, personalize the pitch, and mention the stakes.

Icon 2: **Step 2: Paint the picture.** Brands want to know one thing: How will putting your product on our shelves make us more money or make our customers happier? Give your reps perspective on who will be buying your product. They want to know that you have a lucrative, robust market of engaged buyers in mind.

Icon 3: **Step 3: Explain how the product solves their problem.** Here's where you bring the pitch home. You've explained why you're selling your product and established to whom you're selling. Now you need to establish why they should buy from you. Why is Green Possum, Inc. better than the competition? What is your unique selling proposition?

Icon 4: **Step 4: Respond to objections.** In a sales meeting, there are a lot of things which you can't control, but preparing for objections is one thing you absolutely can control. To prepare for objections, anticipate and proactively address concerns up front. When you acknowledge the objection and empathize with your rep, ask clarifying questions, offer a well-positioned rebuttal, and check for feedback, you are doing your best to successfully respond to objections.

Well, There's Your Problem

Notice how after you introduce the problem, you can move into the steps or tips you're going to teach in the course. This is also a good place to refer back to any previous courses or lessons or ask learners to activate previous knowledge gained. See how using a script, you can introduce your learners to the big problem in an engaging way that meets them where they are and prepares them for what comes next?

STOP HERE What is the Whole Shebang problem your course will help your learners solve? Take a moment now and write down the big problem.

BRAINSTORM SAMPLE PROBLEM SCENARIOS

Once you have in mind the whole problem or whole task you will be showing your learners how to solve, it's time to start brainstorming sample problem scenarios that correspond to the different component skills, steps, and concepts you will be teaching.

> **TIP**
>
> Here you can brainstorm a list of problem scenarios that SMEs, you, or similar learners have encountered related to the whole problem. Remember, brainstorming works best if you don't edit yourself. Just let the ideas flow and see what comes. Also, don't worry about scripting out the problem scenarios themselves just yet. All you're doing now is brainstorming possible scenarios you may want to share in your course.

THE DO IT MESSY APPROACH

For Green Possum, Inc. for instance, suppose your big problem is: How to deliver a sales pitch to big box retailers. Here's a list of possible demonstrations and applications you will want to create problem scenarios around:

- Starting a sales pitch
- Painting the picture for your rep (i.e., making a connection)
- Explaining how a product solves a prospect's problem
- Responding to objection x
- Responding to objection y
- Responding to objection z
- Closing the sale

From here, you can consult with your SMEs about which problem scenarios would most help your learners meet their performance goal and which would be easiest to demonstrate in your course. If you're the SME, then consider which problem scenarios would have helped you the most when you were in your learners' shoes.

When you have done a thorough job of brainstorming, you will have a robust set of possible problem scenarios from which to choose. This is great because the more examples you offer your learners, the better. I recommend that you start with a list of at least 6-8 scenarios to give your learners a wide variety of cases to think through.

Now, it's your turn! Using the following checklist, identify the problem that will form the core of your course blueprint.

CHECKLIST:

- ☐ Review your quick & dirty needs analysis.
- ☐ Identify your performance goal or big outcome. Remember to use the ABCD formula.
    - What do you want your learners to be able to do after completing your course?
- ☐ Identify the Whole Shebang problem that learners will need to solve by the end of the course to reach the learning goal.
    - What real-world problem or task could you use to frame your course?
- ☐ Review your task analysis.
- ☐ Brainstorm a list of sample problem scenarios needed to teach learners how to solve the main and sub-tasks within the whole problem.
- ☐ Consult with SMEs to find out which problem scenarios would be best to address in your course blueprint.

THE DO IT MESSY APPROACH

Student Examples

Example 1: Whole Problem: Setting the Exposure for Crime Scene Photography

Script – Using aperture settings to create crime scene images[14]		
Scene 1 Slide 1	Title slide – Using aperture	**Image:** Image with shallow depth of field. **Navigation:** Start button link to next slide. **SFX –** Background music
Slide 2	**Thabo:** Welcome to the course on using aperture settings in your photography. I am Thabo and I will be your guide for the course. Before you get started, please tell me who you are by filling your name in the text box.	**Continue scene** Text appears in text box
	Navigation: Continue button link to next slide	**Animation:** Thabo appears when the timeline starts on this slide.
Slide 3	**Objectives:** **Thabo:** Welcome [Name], let's begin by looking at the settings you will use to create quality crime scene images with a variety of depths of field.	**Continue scene** Text box appears When the timeline starts on this slide.
	Navigation: Continue button link to next slide.	**Animation:**

---

14 Created by IDOL Dawn Crawford.

THE DO IT MESSY APPROACH

Slide 4	Image of DSLR camera, labels image showing where to find settings for Aperture. Text boxes explain the settings and use. Text: [Name], explore the camera by clicking on the icons to find out about aperture settings. 1. Programme settings 2. Aperture priority 3. Screen 4. Settings **Note:** **Various camera manufacturers name the setting differently and you will find the settings located in different areas. It is best to follow this course with the DSLR camera you will be using to locate where to find the settings. This image is of a Canon DSLR camera.**	**New image** Navigation: Continue button appears once all labels have been visited.
Slide 5	**Thabo:** Now that you know where to set the aperture on a DSLR camera, let's look at how the settings are used to create your images.	Use layers to show a variety of depth of field images.
	Navigation: Continue button shows layers with images and settings. Layer setting Do not hide other layers.	**Animation:** Once all layers have been viewed, the continue button appears and links to the next scene.
Scene 2 Slide 1	Now it's your turn. Use the slider to adjust the aperture settings. When you think your exposure is correct, click on the button to take an image. Feedback text:	Use layers and variables to display images with shallow and deep depths of field.

| | **Depth of field** helps you to isolate the subject of your image from the background. We talk about a shallow or deep depth of field. For example, for an image of the entire crime scene you would want a deep depth of field while for images of each piece of evidence you would require a shallow depth of field. What this means is the entire crime scene will be in focus in the first example (Deep depth of field). But only the evidence item will be in focus in the second example (Shallow depth of field). Use a small aperture opening to get images with a deep depth of field. Use a large aperture opening for a shallow depth of field. | |

Example 2: Whole Problem: Using an AED Machine in an Emergency

Whole Problem[15]
Using the AED Machine in an Emergency at Planet Fitness

  A- PF all staff

  B- Will successfully identify an emergency requiring the use of an AED machine and will use the AED machine

  C- During an emergency

  D- With 100% accuracy and saving a life.

---

15 Created by IDOL Kristin Minch.

THE DO IT MESSY APPROACH

SCRIPTING the PROBLEM

Slide 1: Title/Intro
Title: How to save a life: Using the AED machine during an emergency at Planet Fitness.

Slide 2: Setting the scene
Text box 1: Hello Associate(name)! Thanks for becoming a member of the Clean Thumb Club Team! There's so much to learn, see, and do! But don't worry, we've got your back. Our Veteran team members, Alex, Yaritza, and Patel will guide you as you complete this training course. So let's get this PF Party started! (or may make Alex the narrator)

Text box 2: You may or may not know much about health and fitness, you might work out or not, and that's ok. But like most things in life, we live by SAFETY FIRST! This is where we begin our very important, life-saving training in this course.

Text box 3: As a PF staff member, you are required to become first aid/cpr certified, as well as be able to perform a simulation using an AED machine to save a life during an appropriate emergency.

Text box 4: Staying alive, staying alive!

Slide 3: Introducing the Whole Problem
Text box 1: Here's our crew- Alex, is our fitness trainer and is formally trained to perform the main first aid role in an emergency. He is here mostly during the weekdays, with PE for PF, working with members.

Text box 2: Yaritza is our Asst. Manager. Like Alex, she is also formally trained in first aid. She supervises the staff during the weekdays. But what if a medical emergency occurs at another time? All staff must be prepared and ready for anything!

Text box 3: Patel is a new PF team member like you! You can learn how to perform in an emergency right alongside Patel. If you are unsure as you are going through the course, click on Patel and he will help. (Patel will show up when the learner assessments are done throughout the course)

Text box 4: So, let's stop the chatter and get to learning to save lives.

Slide 4: Activation and Steps Needed to Solve the Whole Problem

At PF, it's a No Judgement Zone. We welcome people of all fitness levels, shapes, sizes, and abilities. We also take into great consideration the differences between our members and we want to be able to meet the needs of any gym member, especially if a medical emergency were to arise. Fortunately, these situations are rare, but if it does occur, we are confident that our PF team will be ready!

Whether it's members or our staff, we want to know with what knowledge and skills you come to us. In order to get to know you a bit more, click on our Trainer, Alex. He's going to give you a little assessment to see what you may already know about using an AED. But don't worry if you do not know anything. Alex, Yaritza and Patel are here to help you.

Icon 1: Introduction to the AED machine with Alex-*Alex will be narrating the information about the AED in icons 1 and 2 in this section.
> "This is an AED machine. (real image and a diagram)
> 1-What do the letters AED mean?
> 2- When is an AED used?"

THE DO IT MESSY APPROACH

Pop up pre assessment for both questions will be included on the Icon Slide

"*Automated external defibrillators* (AEDs) are designed to be user-friendly; with just a few simple steps, you can potentially save the life of someone who has gone into *sudden cardiac arrest. Although the steps to using an AED are simple and user-friendly, there is still a learning curve due to the small differences in the various AEDs found in various places.*"

Icon 2: WARNING- When to use AED
"The first step is to determine whether a defibrillator is actually needed. An AED should *only* be used on someone suffering sudden cardiac arrest, presenting as unconscious and not breathing."

- images- gifs examples pre assess using images that show when to use and not to use AED-Learner chooses yes or no) "How did you do? Are you able to identify a victim when you see it?
    "It should never be used on a patient suffering a heart attack, who is still conscious and breathing." (image)

"If a person is suffering from cardiac arrest, they'll be unresponsive without a palpable pulse, and no breathing or just gasping (in the case of agonal respirations)."

Icon 3: How to make a determination: Hey BUDDY! (Yaritza narrates icon 3-4)
Step 1- While gently shaking the victim, shout the victim's name (or BUDDY if you do not know it) and ask for a response. If there is no response... (this could be a branching scenario?)

Step 2-Then check for signs of breathing.

Step 3-Administer CPR and defibrillation ONLY IF the victim is not breathing and unresponsive.

Well, There's Your Problem

Step 4-A call to 911 would be made by another person to relay the information from your assessment of the victim.
Images to depict each step will be included

Icon 4: Staying Alive!
Steps to using the AED
"These AED steps should be used when:
- caring for a non-breathing child aged 8 or older
- who weighs more than 55 pounds
- or an adult.

Now, let's see what you know!"-end Yaritza

Here is an ordering of the steps for a preassessment....When they put it in the correct order, then they move to the video. They can redo as many times to get it right.
Patel will be the image and assistant for this.

Slide 5- *Video of demonstration of using an AED here as the steps are displayed and narrated by Alex.*
"You Have the Power to Restart a Heart. We Can Show You How."

Are you one of the 50% who can locate an automated defibrillator (AED) at work? With 10,000 cardiac arrests annually in the workplace, you have the potential to save thousands of lives. Immediate CPR and use of an AED can double, or even triple, survival rates. Is your workforce prepared?
Step 1-Complete the *CHECK* and *CALL* steps
- After checking the scene and ensuring that the person needs help, you should ask a bystander to call 911 for help.

Step 2-AED Start-up
- If there are other people available, have them retrieve the AED

95

THE DO IT MESSY APPROACH

- turn it on
- follow the voice prompts

Step 3 - Preparing the victim
- Remove clothing covering the chest
- Attach pads correctly
- If necessary, wipe the chest dry
- Place one pad on the upper right side of the chest
- Place the other pad on the lower left side of the chest, a few inches below the left armpit

Note: If the pads may touch, place one pad in the middle of the chest and the other pad on the back, between the shoulder blades

Step 4 - Using the AED
- Plug the pad connector cable into the AED, if necessary
- Prepare to let the AED analyze the heart's rhythm
- Make sure no one is touching the person
- Say, "CLEAR!" in a loud, commanding voice

Step 5 - To shock or not
- If the AED determines one is needed, get ready to administer the shock
- Make sure no one is touching the person
- Say, "CLEAR!" in a loud, commanding voice
- Push the "shock" button to deliver the shock

Step 6 - CPR
- Immediately start CPR, beginning with compressions

- CPR is done whether the AED delivers the shock, or if no shock is advised.
- Follow the Steps for CPR
- Complete compressions to the beat of "Staying Alive" by the Bee Gees
- Continue CPR until Medical help arrives. "

Slide 6- infographic-AED tips and reminders Yaritza-
*Yaritza will review the key points as the infographic is shown

Slide 7-Your Turn!
Team members! Are you ready to give the AED a simulated try!?
*This is something that they will complete all the steps- can maybe be an actual demo on a dummy, but I'm looking for a game or making one. I'm not sure.

Slide 8-Now you can save a life!
All 3 avatars are on the screen. Each will say 1 thing to the learners.
Not sure yet.

CHAPTER 6

Show 'em How It's Done

Create the Demonstration for the Final Problem Scenario

THE FINAL DEMONSTRATION IS THE most complex scenario you will share with your learners. Ideally, throughout the course, you'll offer a progression of scenarios from simple to more complex that build on each other and teach different component skills (i.e., the steps and conditions your learners need to master to solve the Whole Shebang problem you identified in the previous chapter), ending with the final demonstration. But it's actually easier to start by creating the demonstration for the final problem scenario and reverse engineering the rest of your course from there.

DEMONSTRATIONS OF GENERALIZABLE SKILLS

Recall that in a demonstration, we present general information and show how that general information applies to a specific scenario. Rather than merely telling learners what they need to know, you demonstrate through examples what is to be learned.

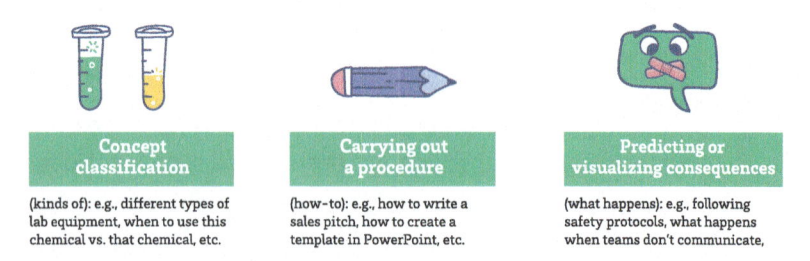

Concept classification
(kinds of): e.g., different types of lab equipment, when to use this chemical vs. that chemical, etc.

Carrying out a procedure
(how-to): e.g., how to write a sales pitch, how to create a template in PowerPoint, etc.

Predicting or visualizing consequences
(what happens): e.g., following safety protocols, what happens when teams don't communicate,

Remember that demonstration works best for three types of generalizable skills:

- Concept classification (kinds of)
- Carrying out a procedure (how-to)
- Predicting or visualizing consequences (what happens)

Take a look at the sample problem scenarios you brainstormed at the end of the previous chapter. Choose the one that is the most complex. It could be a scenario with a lot of steps or a lot of moving parts. This will be your final demonstration.

During the final demonstration you will show your learners exactly how they want the scenario to play out. Even if a challenge or issue arises within the scenario, you will show them how to handle the challenge in the moment. Giving learners the chance to observe the training in action helps them understand what's expected.

Also, you will want to incorporate throughout the final demonstration references to the component skills you've already taught in the course to direct the learners' attention to relevant information. The guidance could come in the form of pop-up boxes, graphics, or videos referring back to the tips or steps you've shared previously. Don't worry too much about the visuals at this point, however. Just make sure to consider the tips and steps as you're scripting your final demonstration. Later, as you create your progression of problem scenarios leading up to this point, you will gradually remove guidance from the application scenarios and by the time you get to the final application, you will have removed guidance entirely.

You may also want to include and ask learners to compare multiple scenarios, relate new information to previously recalled or provided information, and incorporate media that are relevant to the content to enhance learning. Set all of this aside, however, until after you have scripted out the basic content for your course blueprint.

It's not uncommon to spend nearly half of your course on the demonstration (and applications) of the final problem scenario because in many real life training scenarios, the complex scenarios arise more often than the simple ones, and if your learners perform well on the final demonstration, they're likely to have no trouble with less complex scenarios. So it's worth taking your time here.

The biggest challenge with creating the final demonstration is that you're not only teaching your learners to follow a formula or step-by-step procedure, you're teaching them how to think beyond the training. In other words, you are showing them how generalized information applies to specific scenarios with the goal in mind of giving them the skills to apply the information themselves.

In a sales training course, for example, the final scenario might be a how-to or procedural demonstration showing an effective pitch, how to negotiate terms, how to respond to customer objections, and how to close the sale. Clearly a prospect could use any number of negotiating tactics or raise any number of objections, and you can't address every single one in your course. Instead, your goal should be to show your learners how to develop the right skills and mindset to handle similar scenarios.

Here is a final demonstration from the Green Possum, Inc. example introduced previously:

> **Slide x: Final Demonstration - Steps 1-4**
>
> **Text:**
> Now, let's watch Nicole in action one more time as she does a full pitch following steps 1-4. Here she is demonstrating a brand new product line for a rep named Kim from big box store, East Coast Naturals:
>
> **Nicole:**
> Kim, it's good to see you again. I'm excited to be able to show you more of Green Possum, Inc.'s best selling products. Customers who care about the environment also care about what they put on their skin. That's why in addition to our cleaning line with refillable options, we've introduced a line of skincare products. Right now, they're only available on our website, but we're thinking of bringing them to retail. I know skincare is one of East Coast Naturals' biggest sellers and you've been on the frontier of safer skincare. Would you consider being our exclusive retail partner for Green Possum skincare?
>
> **Kim:**
> Well, our customers already love the Green Possum soap refill station and I know they love the scents you carry, so skincare might be another winner. But...it's tough to break into that market. How do I know putting your product on our shelves will make us more money and make our customers happier?
>
> **Nicole:**
> That's a great question! We're prepared to offer every Green Possum, Inc. customer a free sample of our BPA-free sunscreen. [Hands Kim a sample of the sunscreen.] We'll add the samples to current product packages in our next product distribution run.
>
> We know your biggest customer base is moms with kids under five and moms are especially concerned about the dangers of regular sunscreen. And I'm sure you've seen the recent article in *Parenting* magazine about the white-washing of green sunscreen. Many of the allegedly natural brands out there contain ingredients that are banned in most countries outside the U.S. Our sunscreen has been certified as the safest on the market.

THE DO IT MESSY APPROACH

> **Slide x: Final Demonstration – Steps 1-4**
>
> So this will be an easy way to get moms' attention and shift their loyalty from our cleaning products over to the skincare line. With summer coming up, we think this will be a big hit. Our marketing team is also putting the finishing touches on a point-of-sale display to draw attention to the new products.
>
> **Kim:**
> Hmm. We are happy to continue giving you shelf space for your cleaning products, but Health & Beauty is tougher. That area of the store is smaller and we're already running out of space.
>
> **Nicole:**
> I totally understand. There's only so much space in your stores. What if we started with just the sunscreen and you put it in the seasonal section of the store, rather than taking up precious space in Health & Beauty? That would give us a few months to test the product and then make a decision about carrying our other skincare products in the fall.
>
> **Kim:**
> That's a good idea. I've also been meaning to talk to our store designer about expanding Health & Beauty. Those products are always popular with our customers, especially in the Shop Local section.
>
> **Nicole:**
> Good to know. Since all of Green Possum, Inc.'s products are manufactured in our Atlanta, GA facility, we'd love to add our skincare products to the local products section of your Atlanta stores. Do any of those locations have openings for products in Health & Beauty?
>
> **Kim:**
> I'm not sure, but I can put you in touch with our Atlanta rep, Gretchen.
>
> **Nicole:**
> Great! Yes, I'd love to talk with Gretchen. I'll get you set up with the sunscreen samples and a run of 100 units for the seasonal section.

> **Slide x: Final Demonstration – Steps 1-4**
>
> **Advice from Nicole Infographic:**
> **Step 1: How to start your pitch.** Starting a pitch is the hardest part. You have to hook your prospect, so they will actually hear the value of the product and how it will benefit their business. When starting your pitch, you will want to integrate the following: start with the problem, personalize the pitch, and mention the stakes.
>
> **Step 2: Paint the picture.** Big retailers want to know one thing: How will putting your product on our shelves make us more money or make our customers happier? Give your listeners perspective on who will be buying your product. They want to know that you have a lucrative, robust market of engaged buyers in mind.
>
> **Step 3: Explain how the product solves their problem.** Here's where you bring the pitch home. You've explained why you're selling your product and established to whom you're selling. Now you need to establish why they should buy from you. Why is Green Possum, Inc. better than the competition? What is your unique selling proposition?
>
> **Step 4: Respond to objections.** In a sales meeting, there are a lot of things which you can't control, but preparing for objections is one thing you absolutely can control. To prepare for objections, anticipate and proactively address concerns up front. When you acknowledge the objection and empathize with your rep, ask clarifying questions, offer a well-positioned rebuttal, and check for feedback, you are doing your best to successfully respond to objections.

Perhaps you have a philosophy or approach to dealing with certain types of scenarios that works across many different situations. Demonstrate how that approach works and then give your learners the opportunity to practice on their own by applying the skills you showed to a new scenario (more on how to build applications in the next chapter). You could, for instance, script out demonstrations for dealing with two or three of the most common objections learners might hear and

THE DO IT MESSY APPROACH

move on to having learners apply what they have learned to other possible objections.

Notice how this demonstration includes an infographic containing the four steps being taught throughout the course. Your learners may find it helpful for you to end your final demonstration with some additional tips for handling such complex scenarios. After they observe the final demonstration, they will be ready to apply the lessons they've learned.

Can you think of any additional tips to add to the Green Possum, Inc. demonstration above?

SCRIPTING YOUR SCENARIOS

Once you have identified the final problem scenario and thought about the mindset, philosophy, or approach you want to demonstrate, it's time to script out your demonstration. Now, we've all seen awful training videos with laughable dialogue and terrible acting that could have come straight out of an episode of *The Office*. While these training videos may be good for comic relief, they're less effective as instruction. Take those videos as an example of what not to do.

Instead, focus on making your demonstration as close to a real life scenario as possible. Have you seen TV series or films where they add a disclaimer that says, "based on true events?" This is the way to approach scripting your course blueprint and it will take some creativity. But you can draw on your experience and the experience of your SMEs to create dialogue that is true to life. There is nothing wrong with borrowing dialogue word-for-word from situations you or your SMEs have encountered, as long as it's instructive (and you don't reveal any identifying details). Feel free to use these real-world scenarios as inspiration for scripting out your "based on true events" scenarios.

Here are some tips for writing dialogue:
- Aim for a conversational tone
- Use the second-person point of view. Second-person pronouns include: you, your, yours, yourself, and yourselves (From the sample course blueprint introduced in the previous chapter, "Congratulations! **You** just landed a new sales position. **You've** been hired to sell Green Possum, Inc. products to wholesale reps at big box stores.")
- Pitch your script at an 8th grade reading level[16]. Yes, even if you're creating a course for specialists! Anything more sophisticated and you will lose your learners.

Your demonstration should offer a comprehensive solution to the big problem you identified in the previous chapter. For example, you could share a successful pitch to a buyer or category manager at a big box store like Target. Note that you need not have a real-life example to share, in fact, for training purposes, it's often easier to devise a scenario that allows your learners to practice all of the component skills they need to solve the problem. So, instead of presenting the facts and dialogue from a real-life sales pitch in its entirety, consider the components of a successful pitch and create a "based on true events" script that includes those components. It can actually be more fun to make up your problem scenarios. Think of it like writing a play and get creative!

---

16 You can use a tool like www.wordcounttools.com to find your script readability statistics.

THE DO IT MESSY APPROACH

Here's another sample demonstration from an IDOL who created a course about avoiding micromanagement:[17]

> **Slide x: Demonstration**
>
> **Text:**
> Let's watch Kristi [the manager] in action. Here she is having a conversation with one of her team members, Jay:
>
> **Kristi:**
> Jay, how would you feel about presenting our data during the Monday morning meeting? I'm slammed with the new Harper Bakery account, so I could use the help. And I know you're interested in running your own team eventually, so this would be good practice.
>
> **Jay:**
> Wow – sure! But... I'll need some guidance on compiling the data to present.
>
> **Kristi:**
> Of course. Happy to sit down with you to walk you through my process. You'll probably come up with your own system eventually, but I'll show you what works for me.
>
> **Jay:**
> Should I use your Powerpoint slides for my presentation?
>
> **Kristi:**
> If you'd like. But you're also welcome to design your own. And let's meet today to talk more about expectations for the meeting, the big priorities, and updating the meeting agenda. When are you free?
>
> **Jay:**
> I was just about to take my lunch outside. But I can do a working lunch, if now is best for you?
>
> **Kristi:**
> Nope, not necessary! Enjoy the weather, and stop by my office when you're ready to chat.

---

17 This sample course was created by Erica Ashton (though, I changed the names in the script), one of my IDOL course AcademySM students. I'm grateful to Erica for giving me permission to share it with you.

Show 'em How It's Done

Slide x: Demonstration	
Visuals Somehow point out each strategy in their convo. Maybe a "pop-up video" style box appears with each	**Navigation/Animation**

After you complete your script, make sure to explain why the demonstration was successful.

- Were there key steps that you want to point out for your learners?
- What are the consequences of following the procedure according to the demonstration?
- What are the conditions that make this demonstration applicable?
- What properties are important for your learners to remember?

As you continue to build your course, you will refer to the steps, consequences, conditions, and properties in order to reinforce what learners see in the final demonstration. If you leave them to draw their own conclusions about what they just saw, you may not be happy with the outcome.

In the sample demonstration above, you can see how this IDOL made a note in the last row of the table to include visuals that point out key parts of the demonstration she wants her learners to notice. E.g., "**Visuals** Somehow point out each strategy in their convo. Maybe a "pop-up video" style box appears with each." To what is she referring? Prior to the demonstration, she will have introduced some strategies or tips:

THE DO IT MESSY APPROACH

Slide 4: Tips from Kristi

Text
Before you get started, click on the icons to learn Kristi's top tips for avoiding micromanagement.

Icon 1: **Develop your team's talent.** Encourage independent thinking and decision-making. Let them have input, and make time for collaboration and feedback. Learn their interests and strengths. Allow for creativity and ingenuity rather than "we've always done it this way" thinking.

Icon 2: **Delegate**—*especially* tasks that will be repeated in the future, and that connect with a team member's goals or talents. Clarify your expectations, like due dates, deliverables, tools, and priorities, and let them know you're available for questions. Be patient and allow for failure—and when someone succeeds, give credit where credit is due!

Icon 3: **Stay out of day-to-day details.** Give team members space to create their own work processes. Ask for general, big-picture updates, rather than continuously monitoring their behavior. Avoid unnecessary emails or meetings that ask your team to keep you updated on everything.

Icon 4: **Focus on results, not time.** Remember that busyness does not necessarily equal productivity! Efficiency and work processes look different for different people, and your employees may take unconventional routes to get results. Their end products are way more important than time at their desks.

Visuals	Navigation/Animation
Kristi to the side. Icons and text boxes.	Icons visible. Text boxes associated with each icon appear on each click. Previous button to go to previous slide. Continue button appears after all icons have been clicked to go to the next slide.

Show 'em How It's Done

Referring to these tips during the demonstration allows learners to connect the dots and begin to learn important concepts that they will apply throughout the next several scenarios and practice activities. The trick is to figure out how to make these tips memorable and visual strategies can work well here. As you're scripting out your final demonstration and all other problem scenarios, you may want to make note of the visuals and navigation/animation features you will add to your course blueprint later.

Now, it's your turn! Using the following checklist, create the final demonstration for your course blueprint.

CHECKLIST:

- ☐ Revisit your list of sample problem scenarios you came up with at the end of the previous chapter.
- ☐ Identify the problem scenario that is the most complex. This will become your final demonstration.
- ☐ Figure out what mindset, philosophy, or approach you want to teach your learners to help them solve this type of problem.
- ☐ Script out your demonstration for the final problem scenario.
    - Did you use a conversational tone?
    - Did you use second-person pronouns (e.g., you, your, yours)?

- Did you pitch your script at an 8th grade level?
☐ Explain why the demonstration was successful.
  - What tips should you include?
  - What are the key steps?
  - What are the consequences of following the procedure in the demonstration?
  - What conditions make this demonstration applicable?
  - What properties should your learners remember?

Show 'em How It's Done

THE DO IT MESSY APPROACH

Student Example

Demonstration for Final Problem Scenario: Setting the Exposure for Crime Scene Photography

Whole problem demonstration: Exposure Triangle[18]	
Scene 2 Slide 1	**Thabo:** OK [Name], let's get started by looking at the entire Exposure Triangle. The triangle consists of Shutter speed, Aperture, ISO and Exposure Value (EV). Shutter speed is the first aspect we will look at. **Shutter Speed** is used to control the amount of light reaching the sensor and to control the amount of movement shown on the image. You may say to yourself: " ... but I'm a crime scene photographer, why is **Shutter Speed** important to me?" Well, you may not always photograph static crime scenes. The scenes may involve some movement. Imagine yourself at a poaching crime scene where an animal is caught in a snare. The animal will be distressed and moving making your job difficult. But if you know how to capture images where the movement is frozen you will soon become an expert. The next aspect is **Aperture**. Aperture is the size of the lens opening. Aperture is a bit more complex as there does not appear to be any logic between the size of the lens opening and the number used in the setting. The lens opening size is always opposite to the size of the number used to set the opening. For example 22 or F22 gives a small aperture opening while 4 or F4 or lower give a relatively large aperture opening.	**Image:** Blank slide build up the exposure triangle as each aspect is introduced by Thabo who is positioned off to one side.

---

18 Created by IDOL Dawn Crawford.

Show 'em How It's Done

Whole problem demonstration: Exposure Triangle[18]
Like shutter speed, aperture settings are used to control the amount of light that reaches the camera sensor. Small aperture allows a smaller amount of light to reach the sensor. Large apertures allow more light to reach the sensor. Aperture settings also control the depth of field covered by your image. (This will be explained in greater detail later) **ISO** settings talk to the sensitivity of the camera sensor. This setting links back to the SLR cameras that used film instead of a sensor and was a measure of the graininess and speed of the film. ISO can also be used to control the amount of light that reaches the sensor. Higher ISO allows for shorter shutter speeds, Lower ISO's require longer shutter speeds to obtain the desired results. **Exposure Value(EV)** is used in manual mode to adjust the exposure up or down by up to 2 light stops depending on the result of an image taken. This is difficult to use when your desired outcome is to freeze movement. **Job Aids:** Card with Exposure Triangle, Infographic giving additional information about light and light stops can be found in the Job Aids tab..

CHAPTER 7

Give Your Learners a Turn

Create the Application for the Final Scenario

FOLLOWING EACH DEMONSTRATION, YOU WILL give your readers a chance to apply what they have learned. Application of new information provides your learners with opportunities to DO something, such as practice a procedure, play a game, answer a question, etc. This elevates learning from the passive (reading or watching) to the active (applying knowledge). For the final problem scenario, the application will be the part of the course that offers learners the least amount of guidance. It's time to take off the training wheels!

117

THE DO IT MESSY APPROACH

After each demonstration, you should give your learners ample opportunities to apply their knowledge and receive feedback that is corrective, specific, and timely.

PRACTICE ACTIVITIES

Now let's consider some types of practice activities you may want to employ in your applications and what they accomplish. Practice activities prepare your learners to apply new knowledge and skills as well as build their confidence. Here are some types of practice activities:[19]

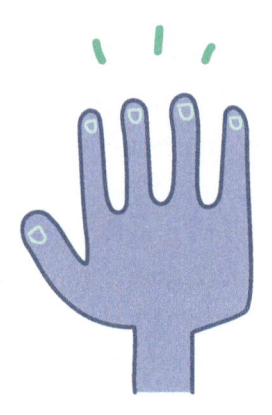

- **Hands-on activities:** Learners use real tools with guidance, such as filling out a form, experimenting with a PowerPoint template, or creating an Excel formula and doing a calculation. The instructor starts out by explaining the purpose of the activity. Then the learners perform each step and receive feedback about their performance. If a learner can't perform a step, they are prompted to go back and review and try again. Finally, learners test their ability to perform the procedure or

---

[19] For more information about application activities, check out M. David Merrill's publications on Instructional Design: https://mdavidmerrill.wordpress.com/publications/instructional%20design/

Give Your Learners a Turn

task on their own. Hands-on activities are best used to teach "how-to" or "what happens" skills.

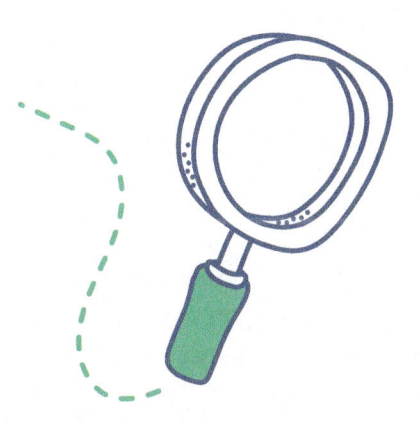

- **Guided analysis activities:** The instructor leads learners through an analysis with step-by-step instruction. For example, an instructor might guide learners through a side-by-side comparison to compare and contrast alternatives or have learners classify items or put them in a hierarchical order. During the activity, instructors should ask questions that provoke deeper thinking, such as, "what's wrong with this?" "how would you correct the error?," and "what would be the result of performing this action?" Guided analysis activities are best used to teach "kinds of" skills.

- **Teamwork activities:** You might also want your learners to collaborate to perform a complex task. Teamwork activities work well when the skills you need to teach require more than individual efforts. Teamwork activities can be used to teach any of the three types of generalizable skills (kinds of, how-to, and what happens) within a team setting.

Keeping in mind your organizational constraints revealed during your quick and dirty needs analysis, here are some best practices for using practice activities:

- Let learners practice as much as they need.
- Ensure that learners apply the right knowledge and skills.
- Do not oversimplify the practice scenarios.

For a sales training course, you could, for example, give your learners a chance to create their own sales pitch, using a guided analysis activity. After they have written out their sales pitch, ask them to compare it to the sales pitch in the demonstration, making sure to reinforce the steps, consequences, conditions, and properties yet again (i.e., with visual components). If you're worried about having too much repetition in your course, keep in mind that repetition of concepts, along with opportunities to practice, is one of the most effective learning methods. Don't overthink this.

Here are two sample applications at the end of the Green Possum, Inc. course:

Give Your Learners a Turn

> **Slide x: Application - Steps 1-4**
>
> **Text**
> Text box 1:
> Now it's your turn. Imagine that Nicole has spoken to Gretchen, East Coast Naturals' Atlanta rep, and booked a sales pitch for you. Your job is to pitch Gretchen Green Possum, Inc.'s new skincare line. You know that the "shop local" section of the store is very popular, and that's good news because Green Possum is an Atlanta-based company. You also know that Gretchen has been looking for a natural skincare line that will be popular with women over 50.
>
> Nicole speech bubble 1: Read this scenario. How would you start your pitch for Gretchen? After you write your answer, compare it to Nicole's sample pitch.
>
> Text box 2: [Learner writes.]
>
> Text box 3 [appears after learner submits their response]:
> Nicole's sample pitch: Hi Gretchen! It's great to meet you. I'm excited to show you Green Possum, Inc.'s brand new skincare line made right here in Atlanta. Now, I know that you're looking for a product that will be popular with women over 50. And our products have tested exceptionally well with this demographic. Not only do they appreciate our natural, fresh scents, but they love the way our products moisturize their skin. Given all of our research, I believe your customers will be excited about our products.

THE DO IT MESSY APPROACH

> **Slide x: Application – Steps 1-4**
>
> Nicole speech bubble 2:
> Is your answer similar to mine? Did you remember Step 1: start with the problem, personalize the pitch, and mention the stakes?
>
> Text box 1:
> Now suppose Gretchen asks, "How will putting your product on our shelves make us more money or make our customers happier?"
>
> Nicole speech bubble 1: Read this scenario. How would you paint the picture for Gretchen? After you write your answer, compare it to Nicole's example.
>
> Text box 2: [Learner writes.]
>
> Text box 3 [appears after learner writes their response]:
> Nicole's example: Great question! Our research shows that women over 50 are most concerned with two things when it comes to skincare: Will it make me look younger? And, will it feel good on my skin? The women in our focus group ranked Green Possum's skincare products higher than the competition on both counts. To get the word out about our products, we've created an ad campaign to target this age demographic and we'll include East Coast Naturals under the "where to buy" section. We believe having our products on your shelves will bring in a wave of new customers to East Coast Naturals.
>
> Nicole speech bubble 2:
> Is your answer similar to mine? Did you remember Step 2: give Gretchen perspective on your product? Did you show her that you have a lucrative, robust market of engaged buyers in mind?
>
> Text box 1:
> "Okay," says Gretchen. "In the past, when we've tested skincare products in our stores, we've found that if customers can't try the product in the store, they will try it at home and bring it back for a refund if they don't like it. This costs us money."
>
> Nicole speech bubble 1: Read this scenario. How does your product solve Gretchen's problem? After you write your answer, compare it to Nicole's example.

122

Give Your Learners a Turn

> **Slide x: Application – Steps 1-4**
>
> Text box 2: [Learner writes.]
>
> Text box 3 [appears after learner submits their response]:
> Nicole's example: Ah yeah, it's really important for customers to be able to try new skincare products in the store. We're happy to provide you with product testers and free samples. Also, unlike our competitors, we will reimburse you for any customer refunds. All you have to do is save the returned products and return them to us. At Green Possum, Inc., we stand behind our products.
>
> Nicole speech bubble 2:
> Is your answer similar to mine? Did you remember Step 3: explain why Green Possum is better than the competition? Did you offer a unique selling proposition?
>
> Text box 1:
> "That's good to know," says Gretchen. "Still, your product retails for about 10% more than our current best selling skincare products. I don't know if our customers will pay more."
>
> Nicole speech bubble 1: Read this scenario. How would you respond to Gretchen's objection? After you write your answer, compare it to Nicole's response.
>
> Text box 2: [Learner writes.]
>
> Text box 3 [appears after learner submits their response]:
> Nicole's response: Yes, we're sensitive to this concern. We're aware of the price difference and we've priced our products really intentionally. Unlike our competitors who cut corners by adding alcohol or water to their products, we use premium quality aloe or natural oils as a base. Our marketing department is working on packaging that highlights this difference. And if you're willing to work with us on product placement, we believe customers will pay more for a superior product. Does this answer your question?
>
> Nicole speech bubble 2:
> Is your answer similar to mine? Did you remember Step 4: acknowledge the objection and empathize with Gretchen, ask clarifying questions, offer a well-positioned rebuttal, and check for feedback

THE DO IT MESSY APPROACH

> **Slide x: Application – Steps 1-4**
>
> **Text**
> Text box 1:
> Now it's your turn. Imagine that Nicole has spoken to Gretchen, East Coast Naturals' Atlanta rep, and booked a sales pitch for you. Your job is to pitch Gretchen Green Possum, Inc.'s new skincare line. You know that the "shop local" section of the store is very popular, and that's good news because Green Possum is an Atlanta-based company. You also know that Gretchen has been looking for a natural skincare line that will be popular with women over 50.
>
> Nicole speech bubble 1: Read this scenario. How would you start your pitch for Gretchen? After you write your answer, compare it to Nicole's sample pitch.
>
> Text box 2: [Learner writes.]
>
> Text box 3 [appears after learner submits their response]:
> Nicole's sample pitch: Hi Gretchen! It's great to meet you. I'm excited to show you Green Possum, Inc.'s brand new skincare line made right here in Atlanta. Now, I know that you're looking for a product that will be popular with women over 50. And our products have tested exceptionally well with this demographic. Not only do they appreciate our natural, fresh scents, but they love the way our products moisturize their skin. Given all of our research, I believe your customers will be excited about our products.
>
> Nicole speech bubble 2:
> Is your answer similar to mine? Did you remember Step 1: start with the problem, personalize the pitch, and mention the stakes?
>
> Text box 1:
> Now suppose Gretchen asks, "How will putting your product on our shelves make us more money or make our customers happier?"
>
> Nicole speech bubble 1: Read this scenario. How would you paint the picture for Gretchen? After you write your answer, compare it to Nicole's example.
>
> Text box 2: [Learner writes.]

Give Your Learners a Turn

> **Slide x: Application – Steps 1-4**
>
> Text box 3 [appears after learner writes their response]:
> Nicole's example: Great question! Our research shows that women over 50 are most concerned with two things when it comes to skincare: Will it make me look younger? And, will it feel good on my skin? The women in our focus group ranked Green Possum's skincare products higher than the competition on both counts. To get the word out about our products, we've created an ad campaign to target this age demographic and we'll include East Coast Naturals under the "where to buy" section. We believe having our products on your shelves will bring in a wave of new customers to East Coast Naturals.
>
> Nicole speech bubble 2:
> Is your answer similar to mine? Did you remember Step 2: give Gretchen perspective on your product? Did you show her that you have a lucrative, robust market of engaged buyers in mind?
>
> Text box 1:
> "Okay," says Gretchen. "In the past, when we've tested skincare products in our stores, we've found that if customers can't try the product in the store, they will try it at home and bring it back for a refund if they don't like it. This costs us money."
>
> Nicole speech bubble 1: Read this scenario. How does your product solve Gretchen's problem? After you write your answer, compare it to Nicole's example.
>
> Text box 2: [Learner writes.]
>
> Text box 3 [appears after learner submits their response]:
> Nicole's example: Ah yeah, it's really important for customers to be able to try new skincare products in the store. We're happy to provide you with product testers and free samples. Also, unlike our competitors, we will reimburse you for any customer refunds. All you have to do is save the returned products and return them to us. At Green Possum, Inc., we stand behind our products.

THE DO IT MESSY APPROACH

> **Slide x: Application – Steps 1-4**
>
> Nicole speech bubble 2:
> Is your answer similar to mine? Did you remember Step 3: explain why Green Possum is better than the competition? Did you offer a unique selling proposition?
>
> Text box 1:
> "That's good to know," says Gretchen. "Still, your product retails for about 10% more than our current best selling skincare products. I don't know if our customers will pay more."
>
> Nicole speech bubble 1: Read this scenario. How would you respond to Gretchen's objection? After you write your answer, compare it to Nicole's response.
>
> Text box 2: [Learner writes.]
>
> Text box 3 [appears after learner submits their response]:
> Nicole's response: Yes, we're sensitive to this concern. We're aware of the price difference and we've priced our products really intentionally. Unlike our competitors who cut corners by adding alcohol or water to their products, we use premium quality aloe or natural oils as a base. Our marketing department is working on packaging that highlights this difference. And if you're willing to work with us on product placement, we believe customers will pay more for a superior product. Does this answer your question?
>
> Nicole speech bubble 2:
> Is your answer similar to mine? Did you remember Step 4: acknowledge the objection and empathize with Gretchen, ask clarifying questions, offer a well-positioned rebuttal, and check for feedback?

Give Your Learners a Turn

> **Slide x: Application – Steps 1-4 (Real World Application)**
>
> **Text**
> Text box 1:
> Now it's time for you to take the lessons learned here out into the real world. Write up a sales pitch for one of your own prospects and role play that pitch with one of your colleagues or your manager.
>
> Nicole speech bubble 1: Now it's your turn. Can you write a sales pitch?
>
> Text box 2: [Learner writes.]
>
> Nicole speech bubble 2: Does your pitch include all 4 steps?
>
> Nicole speech bubble 3: If you need to review the steps return to the infographic on a previous slide.
>
> Now that you have a sales pitch, practice it with one of your colleagues or your manager and ask for critical feedback.

Notice how, in the first application, learners have a chance to write their own reply, compare it to Nicole's sales pitch, and then are prompted to think about the tips provided earlier in the course.

In this hands-on activity, learners are applying what they have seen demonstrated previously to a similar problem scenario. They also receive immediate feedback and are reminded of Nicole's tips, which reinforces what they have learned. In the second application, we ask the learner to apply what they have learned to a real-world case. This is the fullest expression of asking the learner to solve a problem on their own and applying the lessons learned.

THE DO IT MESSY APPROACH

Now, it's your turn! Using the following checklist, create the application for the final scenario for your course blueprint.

CHECKLIST:

- ☐ Review the final demonstration you created at the end of the last chapter.
- ☐ Figure out which type of practice activity (hands-on, guided analysis, or teamwork) will help your learners most in applying their knowledge to the final scenario.
- ☐ Design your hands-on activity, guided analysis activity, or teamwork activity.
- ☐ Script out your application for the final problem scenario.
    - Did you use a conversational tone?
    - Did you use second-person pronouns (e.g., you, your, yours)?
    - Did you pitch your script at an 8th grade level?
- ☐ Make sure that your application covers all the steps, consequences, conditions, and properties covered in the demonstration.
- ☐ Create feedback that is corrective, specific, and timely (e.g., provide learners with a way to compare their responses to ideal responses).

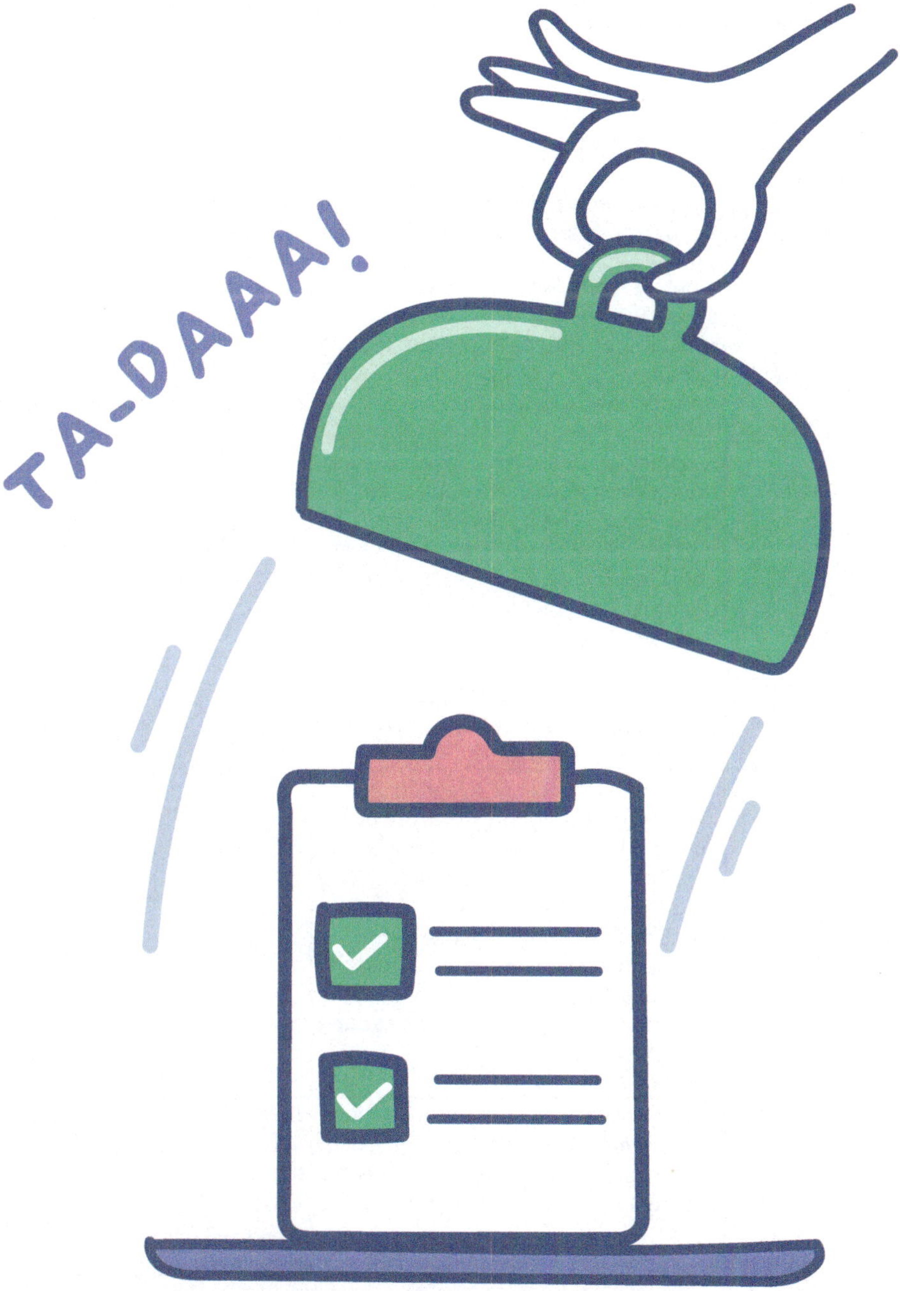
TA-DAAA!

THE DO IT MESSY APPROACH

Student Examples

Example 1: Application of the Final Problem Scenario: Setting the Exposure for Crime Scene Photography

\multicolumn{3}{l}{Whole problem Application: Exposure Triangle - Aperture[20]}
Scene 3 Slide 1	**Thabo:** Now it's your turn. You learnt a little about Aperture in the previous lesson. Now it is time to try out setting exposures to obtain images with your desired depth of field. Remember, in shallow depth of field images only the image subject is fully in focus. The background will be blurred. Shallow depths of field are obtained by using a large aperture opening. This means you need to set a low F-Stop (aperture opening). In deep depths of field images a high F-Stop setting is set to have the entire scene in focus.	**Image:** Camera with screen open, slider is used to set the various settings. Here you can only set the aperture.
	Feedback 5:	
	The antelope is starting to go out of focus but the background is fully in focus. The image is the darkest and you would need to adjust either the shutter speed or ISO to lighten the image. In full manual mode you could adjust the EV value to lighten the images. This can also be done in your post-production phase using Adobe Lightroom or similar applications.	
	Navigation: Click continue to view the camera simulation that will help you to get to grips with the aperture settings.	**Animation/SFX:** When the slider moves to a specific F-Stop a layer is triggered showing the resulting image.

---

20 Created by IDOL Dawn Crawford.

	Whole problem Application: Exposure Triangle - Aperture	
	Hidden text boxes shown through state changes when the layer timeline starts on each layer. **Feedback 1:** The antelope is in focus but the background is blurred. This means you have set a low F-Stop which helps to freeze movement and isolate the subject from the background. As you increase the F-Stop value more and more of the background will be in focus along with the antelope. You will also notice that as you increase the F-Stop value the image becomes darker as less light reaches the sensor.	
	Feedback 2: The antelope is still in focus but more of the background is in focus. As the aperture size gets smaller your image's depth of field gets deeper. But the images become darker due to less light reaching the sensor.	
	Feedback 3: The antelope is still in focus and the background is more in focus. The depth of field is becoming deeper with each adjustment of the F-Stop setting. The image becomes darker as the value changes because less light reaches the sensor due to the smaller aperture opening.	
	Feedback 4: The antelope remains in focus. The image is darker and the background is almost in focus. The aperture opening is getting smaller with each change in setting creating a deeper depth of field.	

THE DO IT MESSY APPROACH

Example: Application for the Final Scenario: How to Verify Income

Slide ___: Application–How to verify income[21]
Text
Text box 1:
Now that you have reviewed the steps to verifying income, it is your turn to give it a try!
Andrea speech bubble 1: You open up some income documentation in Docuware and see you have received the two pay stubs shown here. Can this income be verified? If it can be verified, what would the gross monthly income be? If it cannot be verified, why not? Compare your answer to mine below.
Text box 2: [Learner writes.]
Text box 3:
Andrea's response: Although we received 2 pay stubs for this customer, we cannot verify his income because I can see that the customer is paid weekly. He must send his 4 most recent pay stubs for verification. In some cases, we might be able to use the Year-to-Date (YTD) method, but because sit appears this is a newer job, the YTD method would not give us an accurate gross monthly amount.
Andrea's speech bubble 2:
How did you do? Let's try another example! Below, you will see a Social Security Award letter. Can this income be verified? If it can be verified, what would the gross monthly income be? If it cannot be verified, why not? Compare your answer to mine below.
Text box 1: Remember to review the date of the award letter.
Text box 2: [Learner writes.]

---

21 Created by IDOL Colleen Priester.

Slide ___: Application–How to verify income

Text box 3:

Andrea's response: Although this letter is from 2021, we CAN accept it. However, there is a small calculation we need to make to be sure the amount is accurate. Do you remember what that calculation is?

Text box 4: Learner types answer

Andrea speech bubble 2:

If you said you needed to multiply the monthly SS amount by 1.059 to reflect the 2022 increase, you are correct! The gross monthly income would be $_____.

Text box 1:

Now that you have practiced reviewing income for a few customers, let's review how to document the income.

Andrea's Speech Bubble 1: Since you were able to calculate the SS amount for our customer, Jane Smith, now you will need to document in our systems. Explain what must be done in the following systems:
CRM
MyApp
OSCAR (if there is a record)

Text box 2: [Learner writes.]

Text box 3:

In CRM, it is necessary to update the system with the correct income, then you can verify it. Finally, you would leave a note detailing what you received. For this customer, your note would read:

Received SS benefit letter 2021 for RP (ratepayer), multiplied by 1.059 to reflect yearly increase.

Jane Smith-Self-Social Security-$1041

THE DO IT MESSY APPROACH

> **Slide ___: Application-How to verify income**
>
> For MyApp, you would update the income and copy/paste the note.
>
> For OSCAR, you would copy/paste the note.
>
> Andrea's speech bubble 2:
>
> How did you do? Leaving detailed, accurate notes is so important. If you need help with notes templates, click here.
>
> Text box 1:
>
> There is one final step involved in income verification, and that is indexing in Docuware. Once you have worked a record, you must update a few things in Docuware to ensure the income is connected to the customer's record.
>
> Andrea's speech bubble 1: Explain what information is needed to "index" a record in Docuware.
>
> Text box 2: [Learner writes.]
>
> Text box 3:
>
> Andrea's response: You would need the customer's last name, last 4 of their SSN, and their mailing address zip code.
>
> Andrea's speech bubble 2:
>
> Did you list all 3 correctly? It looks like you have done a great job with these tasks. Now, take some time to complete some additional practice income verification tasks.

CHAPTER 8

99 Problems

Create Several Problem Scenario Briefs

OF COURSE, YOU WON'T PRESENT the final demonstration and application right out of the gate. Remember the activation principle: learning is promoted when learners activate relevant prior knowledge or experience. This reminds us to meet our learners where they are. Again, think of your course as the bridge from where your learners are to achieving the learning goal, and the final problem scenario is the last, hardest part of the bridge to cross.

For this reason, the earlier scenarios you present should be more like a warm up. For the same reason that you wouldn't recommend to someone who has never run more than a mile, that they go out and try to run a marathon, you wouldn't ask your learners to dive into the final problem scenario

THE DO IT MESSY APPROACH

immediately. Instead, the earlier scenarios should be less complex with easier solutions and draw on your learners' prior knowledge.

In this chapter, you'll focus on coming up with several problem scenario briefs that, when placed in the proper order, progressively build on each other and build up to the final scenario you have already created. Start by going back to your list of sample problem scenarios you brainstormed in chapter 5 and identifying one that is easier than the final scenario. Write up a short paragraph to serve as a problem scenario brief. Go down the list doing the same for all of your sample problem scenarios and any additional problem scenarios you might think of.

Don't worry about determining the order of difficulty just yet (you'll tackle this task in the next chapter). You'll be able to more easily decide on order after you have detailed several different problem scenarios. For some of these problem scenarios, you'll create demonstrations as you did earlier. For others, you'll create applications and practice activities that give your learners a chance to apply their skills. For now, focus on crafting a brief paragraph including the major points for several real-world scenarios.

Digging into your problem scenarios in this way will help you begin to see how they will form the scaffolding of your course. Having clear scenarios with enough substance is key to achieving your learning outcome. So, you will need to get creative here!

Here are some sample problem scenario briefs from the avoiding micromanagement course introduced earlier:

99 Problems

> **Avoiding Micromanagement**
>
> **Problem Scenario 1:** You have a kick-off meeting with your first client – a local theater called Waverly Stage. It's the first big mevweting between your firm and Waverly, so impressions are important. One of your graphic designers, Blaine, participates in community theater and referred Waverly. Should you invite Blaine to the kick-off meeting?
>
> **Problem Scenario 2:** Per your firm's protocol, you always design a client's new landing page before writing an announcement blog. However, your team's copywriter, Tabatha, thinks it would be better to write the blog first in Waverly's case. What should you do?
>
> **Problem Scenario 3:** You've just gotten the sign-off on Waverly's social media campaign. The deadline for the first deliverables – Google Ads, blog copy, and social media posts – is two weeks away. How often should you ask for updates on your team's progress?

Notice how each scenario deals with a different managerial challenge and prompts learners to think about how to solve that challenge, so that learners can practice avoiding micromanagement in a variety of situations. Scenario 1 asks learners to consider who on the team should be invited to a client kick-off meeting. Scenario 2 discusses what to do when a team member wants to break protocol or change the timeline. And Scenario 3 asks managers to consider how often to check-in with their teams during a two-week project.

Each subsequent demonstration or application will either show learners how to solve the problem presented in the problem scenario or ask learners to apply the skills they have learned to solve the problem presented in the problem scenario.

Again, in the Green Possum, Inc. sales example, you want your learners to understand the consequences, both positive and

THE DO IT MESSY APPROACH

> **💡 TIP**
>
> Notice also how each problem scenario brief in this example is robust enough to support instruction. Each scenario or problem instance should contain the following elements: consequences, conditions, steps, and properties.

negative, of different types of pitches and ways to respond to objections. Also, you want to make it clear what conditions make one type of pitch better than another. For instance, during a pitch meeting with a busy wholesale buyer, there's no time for small talk or for long, drawn out introductions. You want a simple introduction before getting right into your presentation (ideally, you would have already qualified your prospect during a pre-presentation phone call, so you can move right into your sales pitch). An important part of each scenario is allowing your learners to identify the success conditions.

Additionally, you will provide your learners with the steps needed, in the proper order, to complete the task and each application will give them a chance to demonstrate that they understand the steps you have taught. Each scenario should ask learners to follow the same steps in the same order. The difference is that easier scenarios may not include all of the steps or they may not involve all of the conditions contained in the final problem scenario.

Finally, consider what properties in each scenario will give your learners the best instructional learning experience. Rather than offering obvious, straightforward scenarios, it may make sense to provide problem scenarios that stretch your learners' critical thinking skills. In a sales training scenario, for example, include some common objections and strategies for handling those objections.

Now, it's your turn! Using the following checklist, create several problem scenario briefs covering the component skills your course blueprint teaches.

CHECKLIST:

- ☐ Go back to your brainstorming list of sample problem scenarios.
- ☐ Starting with whichever problem scenario is the easiest for you to write a brief about, create one-paragraph briefs for each scenario on your list.
- ☐ Make sure that each problem scenario brief ends with a critical question.
- ☐ Identify the content elements of your problem scenarios.
    - What are the consequences?
    - What are the conditions?
    - What are the steps?
    - What are the properties?

THE DO IT MESSY APPROACH

Student Examples

Example 1: Problem Scenario Briefs: Setting the Exposure for Crime Scene Photography

Problem Scenario Briefs[22]
Problem 1: You have been tasked with taking crime scene photographs at an accident scene. A large crowd has gathered, including members of the deceased's family. How will you go about taking the images to ensure anonymity of the crowd including the family when capturing the entire crime scene?
Problem 2: You have been called to a poaching scene at a local game reserve. You need to take crime scene photographs that will stand up in court to get the poachers convicted this time. Previous crime scene photographs were of poor quality and led to the criminals being acquitted. What exposure would you set on a sunny day to ensure you have captured the entire crime scene?
Problem 3: At the poaching crime scene you need to capture images of the pieces of evidence found on the scene, e.g. bullets, snares, footprints and the like. What exposure settings would you use to ensure the evidence pieces are the focus of the images?
Problem 4: At an accident or murder scene where you need to be sensitive to family and survivors, what aperture setting would you use on a cloudy day?

---

22 Created by IDOL Dawn Crawford.

THE DO IT MESSY APPROACH

Example 2: Problem Scenario Briefs: Verifying Income

> **Verifying Income[23]**
>
> Problem Scenario 1: You receive a pay stub in Docuware for a customer. They are paid biweekly so you should have received two. The paystub is very recent (June 3, 2022 and the YTD gross is $15,358.45) and you can see that they have been employed for a while. You check the notes in CRM and see that this customer is applying for the customer assistance program. Can you use the Year-to-Date method to verify this income? If yes, then how would you calculate it?
>
> Problem Scenario 2: You receive income for two household members that you can verify. You check CRM and MyApp and see that a 3rd household member has SSI income, but it has not been verified. Explain what you will do in the different systems.
>
> Problem Scenario 3: You receive some income documents that are very blurry. You try to read the various amounts and dates, but cannot see them enough to determine the pay date and the gross pay. What will you need to do with this income? Be sure to discuss how to handle it in all systems.
>
> Problem Scenario 4: You receive a Social Security document, and upon looking in the other systems, you see that it has already been verified in March 2022. What should you do?
>
> Problem Scenario 5: As you are verifying income, you come across several calculation errors made by another Income Specialist. How should you handle this situation?
>
> Problem Scenario 6: You receive an income document for a customer who is self-employed. You are truly unsure if they have sent the acceptable documentation. What should you do?

---

23 Created by IDOL Colleen Priester.

Example 3: Problem Scenario Briefs: Document Sharing

Problem Scenarios:[24]

1. You need to email a link to a document that needs to be signed by an employee. How do you use Google Drive to email a link to someone outside the HR department?

2. You are working on a document with Emory. Rian is your supervisor and needs access to all documents being created and edited by you. How do you add Rian to your documents as a viewer and Emory as an editor?

3. Jade is sharing a document with you to help edit and you get an email notification with a link. She made a mistake when sharing it with you and you get an error message saying you do not have access. How does she fix this?

4. Emory is helping you edit a document with interview questions. However, he is not supposed to have access to the answers given during the interview. How do you remove his access after the document is complete?

5. Rian wants you to share a document you have been working on with Jade, but he wants to limit the time she has access to it because she is moving to another department on a certain date. How do you set up an expiration date for sharing a document?

---

24 Created by IDOL Michelle McCrory.

THE DO IT MESSY APPROACH

Example 4: Problem Scenario Briefs: Accurately Booking Appointments

Problem Scenarios: Accurately place appointments in correct pre-blocked appointment slots[25]

Problem scenario 1: You have all of Tuesdays pre-blocked appointment slots booked. You have an emergency patient calling, crying and begging to come in. *Where should you put this emergency patient?*

Problem scenario 2: The doctor has told his clinical assistant that in July, he's taking the entire week off for vacation. *Who should the clinical assistant speak with next?*

Problem scenario 3: A new patient calls and demands to have their 3rds consultation AND 3rds extraction both done on the same day. The patient says if you cannot make this happen, they will go to another office! *Do you do as the patient is asking?*

Problem scenario 4: A patient calls and describes a lump on their gum directly over where her wisdom tooth #1 is. *What appointment type would this be categorized as?*

Problem scenario 5: The new clinical assistant calls you at the front desk and instructs you and all the other administrative staff to now allow 3rds extractions in the afternoon because so many patients are asking for these appointments. *Do you follow what the clinical assistant is instructing?*

---

[25] Created by IDOL Jamie Black.

CHAPTER 9

It's Easy, If It's Not Hard

Order the Scenario Briefs from Easiest to Hardest

THE GOOD NEWS IS THAT if you've been following along and completing the tasks on each checklist, you've completed the hardest part of building your course blueprint at this point. You've created your final problem scenario and demonstration. You've created the application of that demonstration. And you've sketched out all of the other problem scenario briefs you'll need to build up to that final problem scenario. Phew, you deserve a pat on the back!

The next step is relatively easy – so this chapter gives you a little breather. All you have to do is put the problem scenarios in an order that will make sense for your learners.

THE DO IT MESSY APPROACH

Consider for example, this progression of problem scenario briefs for learning how to create a custom sales pitch deck in PowerPoint:

> **Creating a Custom Sales Pitch Deck in PowerPoint**
>
> **Problem Scenario 1:** You want to create a pitch deck to go with your sales pitch. This will require you to create a PowerPoint template, set up a theme with your brand's colors, and add your company's logo to your template. How will you design your pitch deck?
>
> **Problem Scenario 2:** You have shared your pitch deck with a friend who has a great eye for design. She has three suggestions for improvement. First, use graphics to make your presentation more exciting. Second, create custom animations to keep your audience engaged. Third, create custom slides to give your presentation a more professional appearance. How will you improve your design?
>
> **Problem Scenario 3:** You want to create a dashboard with key stats to share as part of your pitch. Design and create a new slide to add to your pitch deck in PowerPoint including leads generated, revenue increases, number of successful social media campaigns created, and closed sales. How will you create a dashboard with key stats?

In this example, it's easy to see how each problem builds on previous skills learned. Problem 3 is the most complex and requires that learners successfully solve problem scenario 1 and 2.

Some things to consider:
- What skills does each of your problem scenario briefs draw upon?
- What is the level of difficulty of each skill or set of skills? Your SMEs might have input on levels of difficulty, if you are unsure.
- Are there certain skills that your learners need to master before they can move onto other skills?
- Are your problem scenarios missing any key skills?

It's Easy, If It's Not Hard

- Do you need to create additional problem scenario briefs to fill in the gaps?
- Does it make sense to offer scenarios in a chronological order?

Now, it's your turn! Using the following checklist, order the scenarios you've created for your course blueprint from easiest to hardest.

CHECKLIST:

- ☐ Put the problem scenario briefs you have written into the proper order (it may be helpful to put each brief on a notecard, so you can easily move them around).
- ☐ Consider the skills you need to teach your learners to give them the tools to solve the big problem you introduced:
    - What is the level of difficulty of each skill or skill set?
    - Are there some skills that they need to master before learning other skills?
    - Are you missing any skills?
    - Do you need to create any additional scenarios to fill in the gaps?
    - Is there a chronological order that makes sense?

CHAPTER 10

Show 'Em Again

Create a Demonstration for Problems 1-2

NOW THAT YOU HAVE CREATED all of your problem scenario briefs and have an idea of the order in which you will present them, there are just a few more pieces you need before your course blueprint is complete. You have already created a full demonstration

THE DO IT MESSY APPROACH

(and an application) for the final problem scenario by now. But it's also helpful to present a simpler demonstration earlier in the course that illustrates the skills you teach in the first two problem scenarios.

Going back to the Green Possum, Inc. sales example, the first two scenarios are one in which Nicole starts her sales pitch (Step 1) and one in which she paints the picture (Step 2). Each demonstration has a script that touches on each of the skills a salesperson should develop when pitching to big box buyers.

Here are the first two demonstrations:

> **Slide x: Demonstration – Step 1: Starting Your Pitch**
>
> **Text:**
> Let's watch Nicole in action. Here she is starting a sales pitch for a rep named Mac from big box store, Wild Earth:
>
> **Nicole:**
> Mac, it's so nice to finally meet you in person.
>
> Now I know that in the past you've fielded some customer complaints about green cleaning products not working well or smelling as great as traditional cleaning products. And in our research we've found these are the top two things customers care about when it comes to green cleaning products.
>
> Well, not only did Green Possum, Inc. win the Clean Plate Club award for our dishwashing detergent competing against traditional brands, which proves how well our product cleans, but we also have a patented scent that people in our focus groups prefer to other brands.
>
> [Nicole hands over the open bottle for Mac to smell]
>
> What do you think?

> **Slide x: Demonstration – Step 2: Painting the Picture**
>
> **Text:**
> Now let's watch what happens as Nicole continues her conversation with Mac.
>
> **Mac:**
> It smells great, Nicole. But... How will putting your product on our shelves make us more money or make our customers happier?
>
> **Nicole:**
> That's a great question! I know, for example, many of the customers who shop at Wild Earth are new moms. New moms love that our products are versatile. You can use the dishwashing detergent as hand soap. You can even use the dishwashing detergent to wash baby clothes. Since it's all natural, it's great for sensitive skin.
>
> [As she speaks, Nicole demos Green Possum products.] And I should know because I happen to be a new mom. Imagine that I'm at home and my baby just woke up from her nap. I need to wash my hands, but all I can find at the moment is Green Possum's dishwashing detergent. No problem! I wash my hands with the dishwashing soap and am ready to comfort the baby.
>
> **Mac:**
> Hmm. That is an interesting selling point. We could even put your product in several different categories on our shelves.
>
> **Nicole:**
> Awesome! I'm sure you know that new moms are one of the fastest growing demographics when it comes to buying green cleaning products. There's something about having new ones at home that makes us super sensitive to smells and chemicals.

In this case, the first two demonstrations illustrate the main skills of (a) starting with the problem, (b) personalizing the pitch, (c) mentioning the stakes, and (d) providing the prospect with perspective on who will be buying their product. The demonstration should use a similar situation to the later problem scenarios your learners will use as practice, but the

THE DO IT MESSY APPROACH

situation should not be exactly the same. You want to demonstrate how to apply the steps and skills you are teaching without giving away too much.

Because the steps and skills you're teaching in the first two scenarios are the easiest to learn, you can rely on later applications to give your learners the chance to practice these skills. The first two demonstrations show learners how these skills and steps work. They also should activate previous knowledge. Consider building demonstrations that draw on what your learners already know.

Here's another example using the PowerPoint template course introduced in the previous chapter. Recall the progression of problems introduced:

> **Creating a Custom Sales Pitch Deck in PowerPoint**
>
> **Problem Scenario 1:** You want to create a pitch deck to go with your sales pitch. This will require you to create a PowerPoint template, set up a brand color theme with your brand's colors, and add your company's logo to your template.
>
> **Problem Scenario 2:** You have shared your pitch deck with a friend who has a great eye for design. She has three suggestions for improvement. First, use clipart to make your presentation more exciting. Second, create custom animations to keep your audience engaged. Third, create custom slides to give your presentation a more professional appearance.
>
> **Problem Scenario 3:** You want to create a dashboard with key stats to share as part of your pitch. Design and create a new slide to add to your pitch deck in PowerPoint including leads generated, revenue increases, number of successful social media campaigns created, and closed sales.

Here is the demonstration showing a tutorial for problem scenarios 1 and 2:

Demonstration for Scenarios 1 & 2

In this demonstration, we will show you how to create a PowerPoint template, set up a brand color theme with your brand's colors, and add your logo.
 	
Here are the step-by-step instructions:
 	
Step 1: Create the template
  1. Open a blank presentation: **File > New > Blank Presentation.**
  2. On the **Design** tab, select **Slide Size > Custom Slide Size** and choose the page orientation and dimensions you want.
  3. On the **View** tab, in the **Master Views** group, choose **Slide Master.**
  4. On the **File** tab, click **Save As** (or **Save a Copy**, if you are using Microsoft 365).
  5. Under **Save**, click **Browse** to open the **Save As** dialog box.
  6. In the **Save As** dialog box, in the **Save as type** list, choose **PowerPoint Template.**
	Problem Scenario 1: You want to create a pitch deck to go with your sales pitch. This will require you to create a PowerPoint template, set up a brand color theme with your brand's colors, and add your company's logo to your template.
	
	[Learners watch a video walking through each of these steps to create a pitch deck.]

157

THE DO IT MESSY APPROACH

Step 2: Set up your custom color theme 1. On the **Design** tab, click the arrow under **Variants**, and point to **Colors**. 2. Click **Customize Colors**. 3. Click a color box that you want to change. For example, **Accent 1**. 4. Click a new color in the **Colors** dialog box. 5. Repeat steps 3 and 4 for each color you want to change. 6. Close the **Colors** dialog box. 7. In the **Name** box, type a name for your custom theme color, and then click **Save**. The theme color is applied to the current presentation. Step 3: Add your logo as an image Etc.	
In this demonstration, we will show you how to use graphics in PowerPoint, create custom animations, and create custom slides. Here are the step-by-step instructions: Step 1: Use graphics 1. Click where you want to insert a picture or graphic on your slide. 2. On the Insert tab, in the Images group, click **Pictures** and then click **This Device**. 3. In the dialog box that opens, browse to the picture that you want to insert, click that picture, and then click Insert.	**Problem Scenario 2:** You have shared your pitch deck with a friend who has a great eye for design. She has three suggestions for improvement. First, use graphics to make your presentation more exciting. Second, create custom animations to keep your audience engaged. Third, create custom slides to give your presentation a more professional appearance. [Learners watch a video walking through each of these steps to create a pitch deck.]

Show 'Em Again

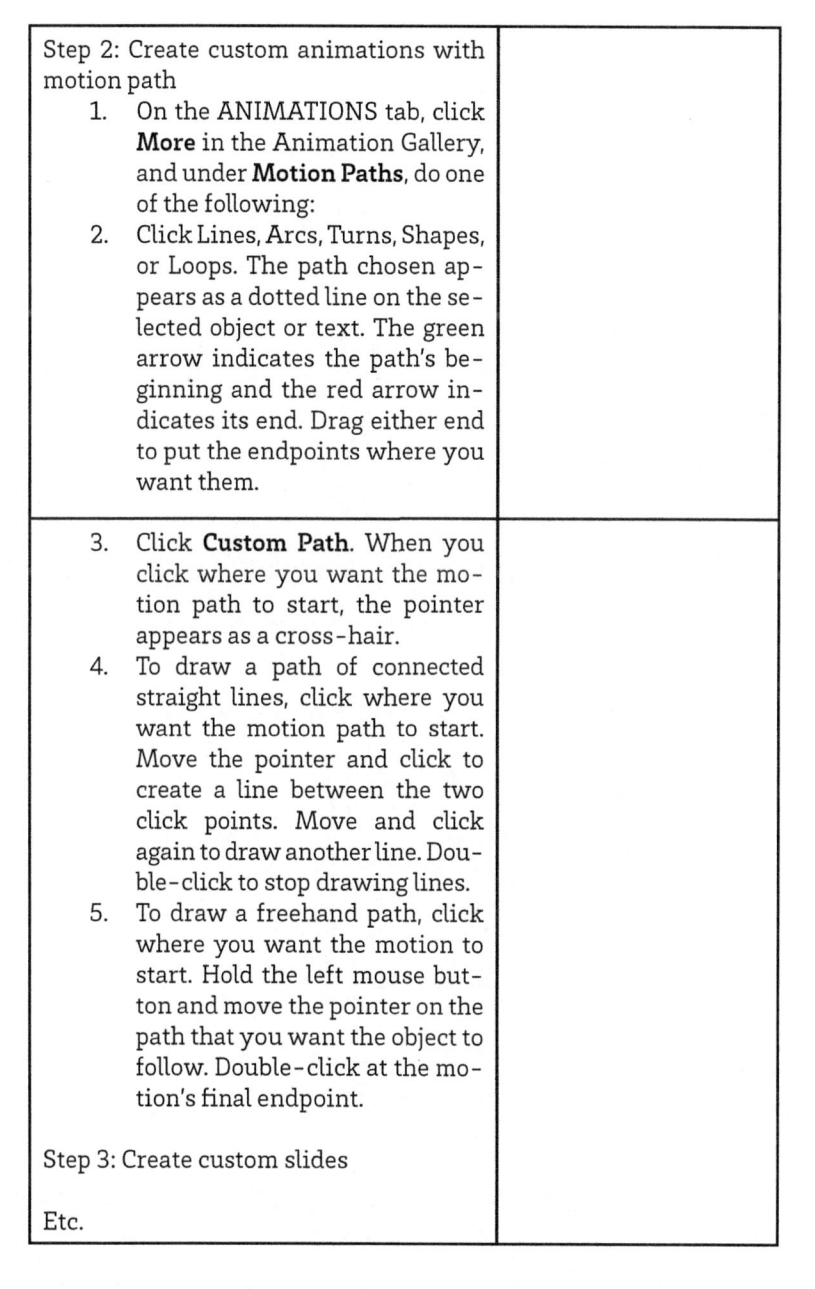

Step 2: Create custom animations with motion path 1. On the ANIMATIONS tab, click **More** in the Animation Gallery, and under **Motion Paths**, do one of the following: 2. Click Lines, Arcs, Turns, Shapes, or Loops. The path chosen appears as a dotted line on the selected object or text. The green arrow indicates the path's beginning and the red arrow indicates its end. Drag either end to put the endpoints where you want them.	
3. Click **Custom Path**. When you click where you want the motion path to start, the pointer appears as a cross-hair. 4. To draw a path of connected straight lines, click where you want the motion path to start. Move the pointer and click to create a line between the two click points. Move and click again to draw another line. Double-click to stop drawing lines. 5. To draw a freehand path, click where you want the motion to start. Hold the left mouse button and move the pointer on the path that you want the object to follow. Double-click at the motion's final endpoint. Step 3: Create custom slides Etc.	

Now, it's your turn! Using the following checklist, create a demonstration for problem scenarios 1-2 for your course blueprint.

159

THE DO IT MESSY APPROACH

> **TIP**
>
> Notice how these demonstrations aren't scripted out like the Green Possum, Inc. sales course or the Micromanagement course. This is partially because of the difference in the content being taught in each course. I wanted to give you the widest possible variety of course examples to show you how the Do It Messy approach works. To make the Custom PowerPoint Template course more fun, of course, the instructor could consider writing a script to go along with the instructional video they create. This is also a good example of how visuals can enhance a course.

CHECKLIST:

- ☐ Identify the skills involved in the first two problem scenario briefs you've created.
- ☐ Reviewing chapter 6, follow the steps there to script out your demonstration for problem scenarios 1-2.

- Did you use a conversational tone?
- Did you use second-person pronouns (e.g., you, your, yours)?
- Did you pitch your script at an 8th grade level?

THE DO IT MESSY APPROACH

Student Examples

Example 1: Demonstrations for Problems 1 & 2: Setting the Exposure for Crime Scene Photography

Problem 1 & 2 Demonstrations[26]		
Problem 1:		
Scene 3 Slide 1	**Text:** Let's join Thabo as he uses a number of well-exposed images to demonstrate how to decide on the exposure to set for your crime scene images. Thabo will use generic images as crime scene images contain sensitive content. **Thabo: (Base layer)** To start off [Name] the image shown was taken on a bright day with the aperture set to capture the entire scene (deep depth of field). When you use a DSLR camera in aperture priority mode, the camera sets the shutter speed and ISO according to the light conditions. You are able to adjust the Aperture to create the desired result for your image. Try to work out what setting was used for this image. In manual mode you would need to set all three aspects of the exposure triangle.	**Image:** Base layer image - Deep depth of field image taken on a bright day.

---

26 Created by IDOL Dawn Crawford.

THE DO IT MESSY APPROACH

Problem 1 & 2 Demonstrations[26]		
Problem 1:		
	Thabo: (Layer 1): Now [Name] look at the image shown. Notice the day is a dull day. Try to decide on the exposure that was used. Is your exposure similar to the one shown on the screen? Remember on a dull day less light will reach the sensor due to the lighting conditions. The only setting changes you will make at this stage is to the aperture setting.	Image: Layer 1 image - Deep depth of field image taken on a dull day.
	Thabo: (Layer 2): This image is an image with a shallow depth of field. [Name] notice how the subject of the image is fully in focus while the background is blurred and out of focus. Remember a larger aperture opening (Small F-Stop) allows you to separate the subject from the background. You know the drill, compare your exposure with the one given for this image. Are you getting the hang of this, let's try one more.	Image: Layer 2 image - Shallow depth of field image taken on a bright day.
	Thabo: (Layer 3): As you did before, look at the image shown. What exposure do you think you will need on a dull day to take an image with a shallow depth of field. Is your exposure similar to the one given on the screen?	Image: Layer 3 image - Shallow depth of field image taken on a dull day.

164

Show 'Em Again

Problem 1 & 2 Demonstrations[26]		
Problem 1:		
	Navigation: Continue button shows layer 1. Each layer has a continue button that shows the next layer. There are 3 additional layers each showing a different image.	**Animation/ SFX:** Text box appears with the actual image settings when the timeline on this slide reaches x seconds. A similar text box appears on each layer to show the image settings when the timeline reaches x seconds on each layer

THE DO IT MESSY APPROACH

Problem 2:		
Scene 3 Slide 2	**Text:** Remember the images shown are generic images as crime scene images have sensitive content, the same principles discussed here will apply to your crime scene photographs. **Thabo: (Base layer)** OK, [Name] remember the first image on the previous slide, it was a deep depth of field image, on a bright day. This image was taken on a bright day but is not as sharp or well exposed as the previous one. The image is quite a bit darker than expected. What could be the problem? Do you have an exposure in mind? Click the exposure button to reveal the actual exposure. If you go back to the exposure triangle job aid, you will notice that it shows how the size of the aperture affects your image by allowing more or less light to reach the sensor. You need to take this into account when setting your exposures. Dark images on a bright day are known as underexposed. You would need to set a lower F-Stop (Larger aperture opening) to allow more light to reach the sensor. Remember the larger your aperture opening, the more out of focus your background will be. You will need to find a happy medium between your desired outcome and the amount of light reaching the sensor.	**Image:** Deep depth of field image on a bright day - Dark (Underexposed)

Problem 2:		
	Thabo: (Layer 1): Let's keep going, [Name]. This image taken on a bright day is overexposed. This means that too much light reached the sensor, overexposing the image. You will need to use what you know about light to correct the exposure. Refer to your job aids to help you. When you are ready click on the exposure button to compare your exposure with the actual one. Did you change the aperture setting to a larger F-Stop? Did you reduce the amount of light reaching the sensor by adjusting the F-Stop to a higher value? If you did then you are starting to grasp setting exposures to obtain your desired depth of field.	**Image:** Deep depth of field image on a bright day - Light (Overexposed)
	Thabo: (Layer 2): This image is underexposed, as it is dark. Do you remember what to do to correct the image? Yes, [Name] you are correct, you will need to set a lower aperture to enlarge the aperture opening. This allows more light to reach the sensor, correcting your exposure and making the depth of field shallower, making the subject more prominent.	**Image:** Shallow depth of field image on a bright day - Dark (Underexposed)

THE DO IT MESSY APPROACH

Problem 2:		
	Thabo: (Layer 3): Light images are said to be over exposed. To correct the exposure in this case, [Name] you will need to reduce the amount of light reaching the sensor. You will do this by setting a higher F-Stop, making the aperture opening smaller. This reduces the amount of light reaching the sensor making the image darker. Refer to the infographic in the Job Aids tab to see how 1 stop change changes the amount of light reaching the sensor.	**Image:** Shallow depth of field image on a bright day - Light (Overexposed)
	Navigation: **Base layer continue button:** Show layer 1 **Layer 1 continue button:** Show layer 2 **Layer 2 continue button:** Show layer 3 **Layer 3 continue button:** Jump to slide X	**Animation/ SFX:** Change the state of the (hidden) exposure text box to normal and the state of the (hidden)continue button to normal when the user clicks the exposure button.

Show 'Em Again

Example 2: Demonstrations for Problems 1 & 2: Verifying Income

> **Slide x: Demonstration – Duplicate Income**[27]
>
> **Text:**
>
> What happens when you receive income, but see that it has already been verified? Watch Andrea walk through the process for Duplicate Income.
>
> **Andrea:**
>
> Ok, I received this Social Security letter for 2022 that shows a monthly benefit of $1205.00. Let me look in CRM to determine if this is the only income necessary for this customer.
>
> (Andrea looks up the customer in CRM and sees that this is the only income the customer has and that it was verified in March)
>
> I can see this customer only has SS income, and I can also see that the same amount was verified in March. I need to look at this customer's record in MyApp/OSCAR to determine if they have sent us the same document.
>
> (Andrea reviews the MyApp/OSCAR record and sees this customer did send the exact same award letter in March 2022)
>
> I am unsure why the customer sent this proof of income again, but since it is SS, it is good for the entire year. I do not need to verify it again.
>
> I will simply create a note in CRM with the wrap code Income Verification Duplicate and state what I received. I do not need to do anything in the other systems.
>
> Had this documentation been a different type or included a different amount, then I would have verified it and updated all systems accordingly.

---

[27] Created by IDOL Colleen Priester.

THE DO IT MESSY APPROACH

> **Slide x: Demonstration – Questions about how to verify income**
>
> **Text:**
>
> There are times when the information sent in may not be easily identifiable, and you may have questions about how to verify it. Andrea will walk you through how you can get answers.
>
> **Andrea:**
>
> This morning, I came across these tax documents for a customer who states he is self-employed. I know that verifying self-employment can be very tricky, and I am not sure I have everything I need to properly verify the income. Fortunately, I have some resources I can use to help.
>
> #1-The Income Specialist Knowledge Base – We have a section devoted to the income chart which shows acceptable income as well as an Income Examples section that shows documents that we may see.
>
> (Andrea will walk through this resource)
>
> I see that I can accept and verify a 1040 and Schedule C for self-employment. That is what I have received. I can also see what deductions I can take out.
>
> I am still a bit confused, though, because this customer will have a negative income when I remove the deductions. I do not see any directions on how to handle that type of situation. So, for this question, I will need my 2nd resource.
>
> #2-Subject Matter Expert (SME)-I will use the Teams chat to reach out to my SME with my question. It is important that I send detailed information in my question. Sometimes, it may be beneficial to request that we discuss via a Teams call so that I can share my screen and we can review the income together.
>
> (Andrea will show a sample chat and how to make a phone call in Teams)
>
> If my SME is unavailable, I can simply skip that record and come back to it later.

CHAPTER 11

Practice Makes Permanent

Create an Application for Problems 3-5

AS THE PROBLEM SCENARIOS BECOME more complex and draw on more difficult skills or a blend of skills, you will want to give your learners ample opportunity to practice the skills you're teaching in the different scenarios you've created. You can return to chapter 7 to guide you through creating more applications for problem scenarios 3-5 and then 6-8 in the next chapter.

The applications you create in this chapter should include scaffolding or guidance to help learners through each practice activity. For example, in an eLearning course, you could include pop up windows reminding learners of the steps or tips you shared previously. It makes sense to offer some hints along the way to avoid throwing your learners in the deep end and expecting them to know how to swim.

THE DO IT MESSY APPROACH

Take a look at the following sample applications from the Green Possum course:

> **Slide x: Application – Step 1: Starting Your Pitch**
>
> **Text**
> Text box 1: Now it's your turn to practice starting a sales pitch. Suppose you know that Mac's customers have been requesting green cleaning products with refillable options. How would you incorporate this into your pitch?
>
> Mac, it's so nice to finally meet you in person.
>
> Now I know that some of your customers have been requesting refillable options [complete the pitch by choosing the correct option].
>
> Option 1 [correct]: Did you know that Green Possum, Inc. is testing refill stations at a few stores? Our research shows that the popularity of refill options is growing among younger buyers (e.g., Millennials and Gen Zers) and I know one of your goals is to attract younger buyers. We would be happy to make Wild Earth one of our test stores. What do you think?
>
> Option 2: Did you know that Green Possum, Inc. is testing refill stations at a few stores? After we do a test run of say two weeks, then we can expand and add refill stations to all of your stores. Our focus group customers really love the refill option. What do you think?
>
> Option 3: Did you know that Green Possum, Inc. is testing refill stations at a few stores? The refill options are self-serve, so you wouldn't need any extra staff to help customers. We would be happy to make Wild Earth one of our test stores. What do you think?

Practice Makes Permanent

Slide x: Application – Step 1: Starting Your Pitch
[Feedback] Option 1: Correct! You started your pitch off well. You started with the problem, personalized the pitch, and mentioned the stakes. Option 2: You talked about the process and mentioned that focus group customers love the refill option, but what about Wild Earth's customers? You didn't personalize your pitch. Try again. Option 3: You didn't refer specifically to Wild Earth's customers and why they might want the Green Possum refill option. You didn't personalize your pitch and you jumped straight into an objection which should be raised later in the conversation, if at all. Try again. **[Advice from Nicole]** **Step 1:** Remember, you have to hook your prospect, so they will actually hear the value of the product and how it will benefit their business. When starting your pitch, you will want to integrate the following: start with the problem, personalize the pitch, and mention the stakes.

Visuals	Navigation/Animation
Text box with three choices. Feedback appears after each choice. **Guidance:** Advice from Nicole shows up with each option to remind learners of step 1. Maybe a "pop-up video" style box appears with each.	Nicole advice appears on icon click. Feedback appears depending on which choice is clicked. Learner can click multiple times. Continue button appears after the learner has clicked the correct option. Previous button to go to previous slide.

THE DO IT MESSY APPROACH

> **Slide x: Application – Step 2: Painting the Picture**
>
> **Text**
> Text box 1: Now it's your turn to practice painting the picture. How would you answer Mac's question: "How will setting up Green Possum, Inc. refill stations make us more money or make our customers happier?" [paint the picture by choosing the best option.]
>
> Option 1: That's a great question! Green Possum, Inc. products are all natural and don't contain any harsh chemicals. Plus, new moms love how versatile our products are. You really shouldn't have any hesitation about letting us set you up with a two-week trial refill station.
>
> Option 2 [correct]: That's a great question! We know for example that younger buyers want refillable options at a higher rate than other generations, by a 2 to 1 margin, and they are value-based shoppers. In other words, they will shop stores and brands that align with their values. They will also trek across town for buying options that are important to them.
>
> Option 3: That's a great question! Refillable options means less waste in landfills and that should make everyone on the planet happier.
>
> **[Feedback]**
> Option 1: You talked about one set of Wild Earth customers (new moms), but you didn't tie that demographic to the refill option. New moms like the versatility of Green Possum products, but do they want refill options? You haven't answered Mac's question. Try again.
>
> Option 2: Correct! You have given Mac perspective on who will be buying your product and provided details to back up your claims. You have also talked about how engaged the potential market of buyers is.
>
> Option 3: You've talked about one benefit of refillable green products, but you haven't painted a picture for Mac about his customers or explained how this option will make his company more money. Try again.

Practice Makes Permanent

Slide x: Application – Step 2: Painting the Picture		
[Advice from Nicole] **Step 2:** Big retailers want to know one thing: How will putting your product on our shelves make us more money or make our customers happier? Give your listeners perspective on who will be buying your product. They want to know that you have a lucrative, robust market of engaged buyers in mind.		
Visuals Text box with three choices. Feedback appears after each choice. **Guidance:** Advice from Nicole shows up with each option to remind learners of step 2. Maybe a "pop-up video" style box appears with each.		**Navigation/Animation** Nicole advice appears on icon click. Feedback appears depending on which choice is clicked. Learner can click multiple times. Continue button appears after the learner has clicked the correct option. Previous button to go to previous slide.

Slide x: Application – Step 3: Explain how the product solves their problem
Text   Text box 1: Now it's your turn. Practice step 3 by considering the following scenarios and choosing the best option for each one.   Customer problem 1: Big box customers are skeptical that green cleaning products work as well as traditional brands, which makes them hesitate to try them. How should you respond? [explain how the product solves this problem by choosing the correct option.]   Option 1: Yes, traditional brands work, that's why they're traditional. But they also work because they include harsh chemicals, which are bad for the environment and sensitive skin.   Option 2: We are happy to supply your store with coupons for Green Possum products, which should entice customers to give them a try. Do your customers like coupons?

THE DO IT MESSY APPROACH

> **Slide x: Application – Step 3: Explain how the product solves their problem**
>
> Option 3 [correct]: Green Possum, Inc.'s dishwashing detergent has won the Clean Plate award. In a blind test against other green products and traditional brands, Green Possum took home the gold medal and we have special packaging that showcases our award-winning cleaning power.
>
> **[Feedback]**
> Option 1: You don't establish a reason your big box rep should carry your product or how Green Possum solves your customer's problem. Try again.
>
> Option 2: Coupons may be able to solve a problem with the cost of your products. However, the customer problem in this scenario is not about how green products are more expensive than traditional cleaning products. It's about how well they work. Try again.
>
> Option 3: Correct! The Clean Plate club award is a unique selling proposition for Green Possum and it solves your customer's problem.
>
> Customer Problem 2: Environmentally conscious consumers – especially younger shoppers – don't want to buy cleaning products in plastic bottles. They see this as wasteful since a lot of plastic can't be recycled. How should you respond?
>
> Option 1: Well, I'm not sure what the alternative might be. Sure, plastics are a problem, but there's really no other way to package some of our products.
>
> Option 2 [correct]: Right, for this reason, we're rolling out refill stations. We're the first in our industry to do so. We believe refill stations would be a great fit for your customers because you have a lot of stores in college towns where research shows there's a high demand for refillable products.
>
> Option 3: While we are rolling out refill stations, we have no immediate plans to go totally plastic free. We find that a lot of our customers are okay with buying plastic bottles as long as they can be recycled.

Slide x: Application – Step 3: Explain how the product solves their problem	
<div>**[Feedback]** Option 1: Even if you can't think of a solution to the problem, you need to give your customer a reason to buy from you. This response makes you seem really inflexible. Try again. Option 2: Correct! You raise a unique selling proposition for Green Possum that solves your customer's problem. You also explain why it's right for their stores. Option 3: You offer a partial solution to your customer's problem here in bringing up the refill stations. But you don't talk about it as a unique selling proposition or position it as a solution. Also, you don't respond to the customer's concern about a lot of plastic not being recyclable. Try again. **[Advice from Nicole]** **Step 3: Explain how the product solves their problem.** Here's where you bring the pitch home. You've explained why you're selling your product and established to whom you're selling. Now you need to establish why they'd buy from you. Why is Green Possum, Inc. better than the competition? What is your unique selling proposition?</div>	
Visuals Text box with three choices. Feedback appears after each choice. **Guidance:** Advice from Nicole shows up with each option to remind learners of step 3. Maybe a "pop-up video" style box appears with each.	**Navigation/Animation** Nicole advice appears on icon click. Feedback appears depending on which choice is clicked. Learner can click multiple times. Continue button appears after the learner has clicked the correct option. Previous button to go to previous slide.

Notice that these applications use a multiple-choice strategy. For each application exercise, learners are prompted to choose one of three options. While multiple-choice isn't always the best mode of practice, this type of long-form answer forces learners to think carefully about what they have learned. The notes below each text box show what guidance will be presented along with each option. You could use a "pop-up video" style box reminding learners about the relevant step, for instance.

Alternatively, you can include a single application that covers all of the skills included in problem scenarios 3-5, or for more complex skills, you could give your learners a practice activity that drills them on a single skill. Remember that application sections give learners the opportunity to practice the skill, rather than passively observing. This is where the real learning takes place.

Here's another example, continuing on with the PowerPoint course from earlier:

Practice Makes Permanent

	Guided Application for Problem Scenario 3	
1	Previously, you watched a demonstration showing you how to use graphics to make your PowerPoint presentation more exciting and how to create custom animations to keep your audience engaged. In this scenario, you will be given the step-by-step guidance and asked to practice with the project files provided. If you get stuck, go back to the demonstration video and rewatch the parts that are unclear. In this scenario, you will practice using graphics and custom animation.	
2	Step 1: Use graphics 1. Click next to the header on the first slide, to insert a picture of the cleaning supply on your slide. 2. On the **Insert** tab, in the **Images** group, click **Pictures** and then click **This Device**. 3. In the dialog box that opens, browse to the cleaning supply picture that you want to insert, click that picture, and then click Insert.	[Provide learners with the problem scenario here.] [Provide learners with the information they need to complete the application here.] [Provide learners with the project file, an interactive PowerPoint presentation without graphics or animations, here.]
	Step 2: Create custom animations with motion path 1. On the ANIMATIONS tab, click **More** in the Animation Gallery, and under **Motion Paths**, do the following:	

181

THE DO IT MESSY APPROACH

	2. Click **Lines**. The path chosen appears as a dotted line on the selected object or text. The green arrow indicates the path's beginning and the red arrow indicates its end. Drag either end to create a line that will "throw" the wholesale price from the top right to the bottom left.
	Step 3: Create another custom animations with motion path
	   1. On the ANIMATIONS tab, click **More** in the Animation Gallery, and under **Motion Paths**, do the following:
	   2. Click **Custom Path**. When you click where you want the motion path to start, the pointer appears as a cross-hair.
	   3. Draw a freehand path, by clicking at the top left, where you want the motion to start. Hold the left mouse button and move the pointer on the path that you want the object to follow, down to the bottom right. Double-click at the motion's final endpoint.	

3	If your Powerpoint does not look like the sample provided, you may want to try again or rewatch the demonstration.	[Final PowerPoint with graphics and animations completed correctly is shown here.]

The two above examples show two different ways to provide an application or practice activity with guidance, giving learners the opportunity to practice what they have learned in a way that makes them feel comfortable. In the next chapter, we'll see what happens when we remove guidance.

Now, it's your turn! Using the following checklist, create an application for problem scenarios 3-5 for your course blueprint.

CHECKLIST:

- ☐ Consider the skills you want your learners to practice in problem scenarios 3-5
- ☐ Reviewing chapter 7, script out your application for problem scenarios 3-5.
  - Did you use a conversational tone?
  - Did you use second-person pronouns (e.g., you, your, yours)?
  - Did you pitch your script at an 8th grade level?

THE DO IT MESSY APPROACH

Student Examples

Example 1: Applications for Problems 3 & 4: Setting the Exposure for Crime Scene Photography

Application Problems 3 & 4[28]	
Problem 3	
Application will take the form of a drag and drop interaction. The learner will categorize images into their correct category namely: Over exposed; Under exposed; Shallow depth of field; Deep depth of field. Correct or incorrect feedback will be given after each drop.	**Image:** Blank slide with a stack of images to drop on the target areas.
Feedback: **Correct text:** Well done[Name], you are able to identify (Under/Over exposed images); (Shallow/Deep depth of field images). Separate correct layers for each category.	
Feedback: **Incorrect text:** You haven't got that correct, [Name]. You are not able to identify (Under/Over exposed images); (Shallow/Deep depth of field images). Separate correct layers for each category.	

---

28 Created by IDOL Dawn Crawford.

THE DO IT MESSY APPROACH

Problem 4		
	Application will take the form of a multiple choice quiz with feedback per question. Questions will be in the forms of images, choices will be 4 x exposures. Learner will choose an answer and receive feedback. Learners are allowed 3 tries.	**Image:** Each question background will be an image with either a Shallow depth of field or Deep depth of field. Choices will be in a rectangle and will be a variety of exposures to choose from.
	Correct Feedback: **Thabo:** That's correct [Name]. You have got to grips with setting exposures using your camera's aperture settings. This is a case of Shallow depth of field / Deep depth of field.	
	Incorrect Feedback: That's not quite right, [Name]. You haven't managed to select the correct exposure. This is a case of Shallow depth of field / Deep depth of field.(A the case may be.)	

Practice Makes Permanent

Example 2: Application for Problems 3-5: Creating a Group in Microsoft Teams

Application with guidance problem scenario 3[29]	
Previously, you watched a demonstration showing you how to create a group on Teams. In this scenario, you will be given step-by-step guidance and asked to create a similar staff group for the business English teachers. (list of members to be added is provided) If you get stuck, go back to the demonstration video and rewatch the parts that are unclear.	

Step 1: Create the Team
 	
1. Open Teams.
2. **Click on the Teams icon** on the left-hand side of the screen.
3. You should see any teams that already exist. Find and click on the *Join or create team* **button** in the top right-hand corner.
4. A series of icons will come up, i.e. join a team or create a team. Click on **create a team**.
5. Now you will see a window with different types of teams, ie class, staff, etc. Click on **staff**.
6. In the pop-up window, fill in the sections you see.
   a. **Name:** ie business English teachers June 2022
   b. **Description:** skip for now
   c. **Privacy:** choose *private-only team owners can add members*
	Refer to the demonstration video as needed OR provide learners with screenshots
	
	[Provide learners with a list of business English teachers.]
	
	Refer to the demonstration video as needed OR provide learners with screenshots

Check to see that your group looks similar to the group we set up in the demonstration video (link provided).	[Link to Teams group set up for general English teachers
Check to see that your group looks similar to the sample class (link provided).	[Link to sample class group set up)

---

29 Created by IDOL Rachel Owens.

THE DO IT MESSY APPROACH

Application with guidance problem scenario 4	
Previously, you watched a demonstration showing you how to create a group on Teams. In this scenario, you will be given step-by-step guidance and asked to create a different type of group— a class group- (class list provided) If you get stuck, go back to the demonstration video and rewatch the parts that are unclear.	

Step 1: Create the Team
 	
1. Open Teams.
2. **Click on the Teams icon** on the left-hand side of the screen.
3. You should see any teams that already exist. Find and click on the *Join or create team* **button** in the top right-hand corner.
4. A series of icons will come up, i.e. join a team or create a team. Click on **create a team**.
5. Now you will see a window with different types of teams, ie class, staff, etc. Click on **class**.
6. In the pop-up window, fill in the sections you see.
   a. **Name:** ie level B1 June 2022
   b. **Description:** skip for now
   c. **Privacy:** choose *private-only team owners can add members*
	Refer to the demonstration video as needed OR provide learners with screenshots
	
	[Provide learners with the class list)

Step 2: Add members to the team (or click on skip to save for later) 1. A pop-up window will come up. In the space that says start *typing a name or group*, type in the names of the new staff members. If they are already in the system, they will pop up automatically. Click to select. The name of the person will appear on the line where you are typing. If they don't pop up automatically, you can type in their emails. 2. When you have finished, click the **add** button on the right-hand side.	 Refer to the demonstration video as needed OR provide learners with screenshots

188

Practice Makes Permanent

Application with guidance problem scenario 4	
Step 3: Choose an icon for your team 1. Teams will generate an icon automatically. 2. To change the icon, enter the new team. You will see the auto generated icon on the left. 3. Click on the **three dots** to the right of the small icon. A dropdown menu will appear. 4. Click on **edit team**. A series of icons will appear. 5. Choose one of the icons or upload your own image in the first box that says upload.	
Check to see that your group looks similar to the sample class (link provided).	[Link to sample class group set up)

Application with guidance problem scenario 5	
Previously, you watched a demonstration showing you how to create a group on Teams and created a staff group and a class group with guidance. The boss has created icons with our logo and the class level for all classes and wants to replace the Teams icons with our logo. In this scenario, you will be asked to change the icon on the class group you created in the last problem scenario. (logo provided) If you get stuck, go back to the demonstration video and rewatch the parts that are unclear.	
1. Enter your class team. You will see the auto generated icon on the left. 2. Click on the **three dots** to the right of the small icon. A dropdown menu will appear. 3. Click on **edit team**. The first box before the icons allows you to drag and drop an image or select a file from your computer. 4. Upload the logo in the first box that says upload.	Refer to the demonstration video as needed OR provide learners with screenshots Provide learners with logo image
Check to see that your group looks similar to the sample class (link provided).	[Link to sample class group set up)

189

CHAPTER 12

End of the Line

Create an Application for Problems 6-8 that Provides No Guidance

FINALLY, YOU WILL DESIGN APPLICATIONS for problem scenarios 6-8. This process will be similar to what you did in the previous chapter. The only difference is that this time, you won't provide your learners with any help. Now is their time to shine. They are ready to take what you've taught them and apply it to their own work and lives.

Here are two final examples showing how learners apply everything you've taught them to the final scenarios without any guidance or help:

THE DO IT MESSY APPROACH

> **Slide x: Application - Steps 1-4**
>
> **Text**
> Text box 1:
> Now it's your turn. Imagine that Nicole has spoken to Gretchen, East Coast Naturals' Atlanta rep, and booked a sales pitch for you. Your job is to pitch Gretchen Green Possum, Inc.'s new skincare line. You know that the Shop Local section of the store is very popular and that's good news because Green Possum is an Atlanta-based company. You also know that Gretchen has been looking for a natural skincare line that will be popular with women over 50.
>
> Nicole speech bubble 1: Read this scenario. How would you start your pitch for Gretchen? After you write your answer, click submit and compare it to Nicole's sample pitch.
>
> Text box 2: [Learner writes.]
>
> Text box 3 [appears after learner has submitted their response]:
> Nicole's sample pitch: Hi Gretchen! It's great to meet you. I'm excited to show you Green Possum, Inc.'s brand new skincare line made right here in Atlanta. Now, I know that you're looking for a product that will be popular with women over 50. And our products have tested exceptionally well with this demographic. Not only do they appreciate our natural, fresh scents, but they love the way our products moisturize their skin. Given all of our research, I believe your customers will be excited about our products.
> Nicole speech bubble 2:
> Is your answer similar to mine? Did you remember step 1: start with the problem, personalize the pitch, and mention the stakes?
>
> Text box 1:
> Now suppose Gretchen asks, "How will putting your product on our shelves make us more money or make our customers happier?"
>
> Nicole speech bubble 1: Read this scenario. How would you paint the picture for Gretchen? After you write your answer, click submit and compare it to Nicole's example.

> **Slide x: Application – Steps 1-4**
>
> Text box 2: [Learner writes.]
>
> Text box 3 [appears after learner has submitted their response]: Nicole's example: Great question! Our research shows that women over 50 are most concerned with two things when it comes to skincare: Will it make me look younger? And, will it feel good on my skin? The women in our focus group ranked Green Possum's skincare products higher than the competition on both counts. To get the word out about our products, we've created an ad campaign to target this age demographic and we'll include East Coast Naturals under the "where to buy" section. We believe having our products on your shelves will bring in a wave of new customers to East Coast Naturals.
>
> Nicole speech bubble 2:
> Is your answer similar to mine? Did you remember step 2: give Gretchen perspective on your product? Did you show her that you have a lucrative, robust market of engaged buyers in mind?
> Text box 1:
> "Okay," says Gretchen. "In the past, when we've tested skincare products in our stores, we've found that if customers can't try the product in the store, they will try it at home and bring it back for a refund if they don't like it. This costs us money."
>
> Nicole speech bubble 1: Read this scenario. How does your product solve Gretchen's problem? After you write your answer, click submit and compare it to Nicole's example.
>
> Text box 2: [Learner writes.]
>
> Text box 3 [appears after learner has submitted their response]: Nicole's example: Ah yeah, it's really important for customers to be able to try new skincare products in the store. We're happy to provide you with product testers and free samples. Also, unlike our competitors, we will reimburse you for any customer refunds. All you have to do is save the returned products and return them to us. At Green Possum, Inc., we stand behind our products.

THE DO IT MESSY APPROACH

> **Slide x: Application – Steps 1–4**
>
> Nicole speech bubble 2:
> Is your answer similar to mine? Did you remember step 3: explain why Green Possum is better than the competition? Did you offer a unique selling proposition?
>
> Text box 1:
> "That's good to know," says Gretchen. "Still, your product retails for about 10% more than our current best selling skincare products. I don't know if our customers will pay more."
>
> Nicole speech bubble 1: Read this scenario. How would you respond to Gretchen's objection? After you write your answer, click submit and compare it to Nicole's response.
>
> Text box 2: [Learner writes.]
>
> Text box 3 [appears after learner has submitted their response]:
> Nicole's response: Yes, we're sensitive to this concern. We're aware of the price difference and we've priced our products really intentionally. Unlike our competitors who cut corners by adding alcohol or water to their products, we use premium quality aloe or natural oils as a base. Our marketing department is working on packaging that highlights this difference. And if you're willing to work with us on product placement, we believe customers will pay more for a superior product. Does this answer your question?
>
> Nicole speech bubble 2:
> Is your answer similar to mine? Did you remember step 4: acknowledge the objection and empathize with Gretchen, ask clarifying questions, offer a well-positioned rebuttal, and check for feedback?

End of the Line

Slide x: Application – Steps 1-4	
Visuals Office background with three text boxes—1 top and centered, 2 below one and to the left, 3 aligned with 2 and to the right: | 1 | | 2 | 3 | Nicole appears to the right of 3, gesturing to the answer with a speech bubble. **No Guidance**	**Navigation/Animation** 1 & 2 always appear. Nicole's speech bubble 1 is visible at first. Text in 3 and Nicole's speech bubble 2 only appear after the learner writes in 2 and clicks "submit." Continue button appears after the learner has clicked Submit. Previous button to go to previous slide.

Slide x: Application – Steps 1-4
Text   Text box 1:   Now it's your turn. Imagine that Nicole has spoken to Gretchen, East Coast Naturals' Atlanta rep, and booked a sales pitch for you. Your job is to pitch Gretchen Green Possum, Inc.'s new skincare line. You know that the Shop Local section of the store is very popular and that's good news because Green Possum is an Atlanta-based company. You also know that Gretchen has been looking for a natural skincare line that will be popular with women over 50.
Nicole speech bubble 1: Read this scenario. How would you start your pitch for Gretchen? After you write your answer, click submit and compare it to Nicole's sample pitch.   Text box 2: [Learner writes.]

195

THE DO IT MESSY APPROACH

> **Slide x: Application - Steps 1-4**
>
> Text box 3 [appears after learner has submitted their response]:
> Nicole's sample pitch: Hi Gretchen! It's great to meet you. I'm excited to show you Green Possum, Inc.'s brand new skincare line made right here in Atlanta. Now, I know that you're looking for a product that will be popular with women over 50. And our products have tested exceptionally well with this demographic. Not only do they appreciate our natural, fresh scents, but they love the way our products moisturize their skin. Given all of our research, I believe your customers will be excited about our products.
>
> Nicole speech bubble 2:
> Is your answer similar to mine? Did you remember step 1: start with the problem, personalize the pitch, and mention the stakes?
>
> Text box 1:
> Now suppose Gretchen asks, "How will putting your product on our shelves make us more money or make our customers happier?"
>
> Nicole speech bubble 1: Read this scenario. How would you paint the picture for Gretchen? After you write your answer, click submit and compare it to Nicole's example.
>
> Text box 2: [Learner writes.]
>
> Text box 3 [appears after learner has submitted their response]:
> Nicole's example: Great question! Our research shows that women over 50 are most concerned with two things when it comes to skincare: Will it make me look younger? And, will it feel good on my skin? The women in our focus group ranked Green Possum's skincare products higher than the competition on both counts. To get the word out about our products, we've created an ad campaign to target this age demographic and we'll include East Coast Naturals under the "where to buy" section. We believe having our products on your shelves will bring in a wave of new customers to East Coast Naturals.
>
> Nicole speech bubble 2:
> Is your answer similar to mine? Did you remember step 2: give Gretchen perspective on your product? Did you show her that you have a lucrative, robust market of engaged buyers in mind?

End of the Line

> **Slide x: Application – Steps 1-4**
>
> Text box 1:
> "Okay," says Gretchen. "In the past, when we've tested skincare products in our stores, we've found that if customers can't try the product in the store, they will try it at home and bring it back for a refund if they don't like it. This costs us money."
>
> Nicole speech bubble 1: Read this scenario. How does your product solve Gretchen's problem? After you write your answer, click submit and compare it to Nicole's example.
>
> Text box 2: [Learner writes.]
>
> Text box 3 [appears after learner has submitted their response]: Nicole's example: Ah yeah, it's really important for customers to be able to try new skincare products in the store. We're happy to provide you with product testers and free samples. Also, unlike our competitors, we will reimburse you for any customer refunds. All you have to do is save the returned products and return them to us. At Green Possum, Inc., we stand behind our products.
>
> Nicole speech bubble 2:
> Is your answer similar to mine? Did you remember step 3: explain why Green Possum is better than the competition? Did you offer a unique selling proposition?
>
> Text box 1:
> "That's good to know," says Gretchen. "Still, your product retails for about 10% more than our current best selling skincare products. I don't know if our customers will pay more."
>
> Nicole speech bubble 1: Read this scenario. How would you respond to Gretchen's objection? After you write your answer, click submit and compare it to Nicole's response.
>
> Text box 2: [Learner writes.]

THE DO IT MESSY APPROACH

Slide x: Application – Steps 1-4
Text box 3 [appears after learner has submitted their response]: Nicole's response: Yes, we're sensitive to this concern. We're aware of the price difference and we've priced our products really intentionally. Unlike our competitors who cut corners by adding alcohol or water to their products, we use premium quality aloe or natural oils as a base. Our marketing department is working on packaging that highlights this difference. And if you're willing to work with us on product placement, we believe customers will pay more for a superior product. Does this answer your question? Nicole speech bubble 2: Is your answer similar to mine? Did you remember step 4: acknowledge the objection and empathize with Gretchen, ask clarifying questions, offer a well-positioned rebuttal, and check for feedback?

Visuals	Navigation/Animation
Office background with three text boxes—1 top and centered, 2 below one and to the left, 3 aligned with 2 and to the right: ``` ┌─────────────────┐ │ 1 │ ├────────┬────────┤ │ 2 │ 3 │ │ │ │ └────────┴────────┘ ``` Nicole appears to the right of 3, gesturing to the answer with a speech bubble. **No Guidance**	1 & 2 always appear. Nicole's speech bubble 1 is visible at first. Text in 3 and Nicole's speech bubble 2 only appear after the learner writes in 2 and clicks "submit." Continue button appears after the learner has clicked Submit. Previous button to go to previous slide.

End of the Line

Slide x: Application – Steps 1-4 (Real World Application)	
Text Text box 1: Now it's time for you to take the lessons learned here out into the real world. Write up a sales pitch for one of your own prospects and role play that pitch with one of your colleagues or your manager. Nicole speech bubble 1: Now it's your turn. Can you write a sales pitch? Text box 2: [Learner writes.] Nicole speech bubble 2: Does your pitch include all 4 steps? Nicole speech bubble 3: If you need to review the steps return to the infographic on a previous slide. Now that you have a sales pitch, practice it with one of your colleagues or your manager and ask for critical feedback.	
Visuals Office background with three text boxes—1 top and centered, 2 below one and to the left, 3 aligned with 2 and to the right: ┌─────────────┐ │ 1 │ ├──────┬──────┤ │ 2 │ 3 │ └──────┴──────┘ Nicole appears to the right of 3, gesturing to the answer with a speech bubble. **No Guidance**	**Navigation/Animation** 1 & 2 always appear. Nicole's speech bubble 1 is visible at first. Text in 3 and Nicole's speech bubble 2 only appear after the learner writes in 2 and clicks "submit." Continue button appears after the learner has clicked Submit. Previous button to go to previous slide.

Notice how in the first application above, Nicole's answers only show up after learners write their own answers and click "submit." Also, the visual notes express that learners are

THE DO IT MESSY APPROACH

prompted to write their answers with no guidance and then compare their answers to Nicole's "ideal" answer as a means of providing immediate feedback. This is a good technique to use for qualitative, long-form type answers.

Here is another example using the PowerPoint template course:

	Application for Problem Scenario 6 with No Guidance	
1	In the previous scenarios, you were guided step-by-step in the application of commands to complete the practice activity. In this scenario, you will not be given this step-by-step guidance. You should review the steps provided earlier, then you should try to complete the steps in each task on your own. If you need help, there is learner guidance provided at the end of each task. You will learn more if you try to perform each task before looking at the guidance and only use the guidance when you are unable to perform the required commands. After each task, you will be shown a sample PowerPoint with the task done correctly. In this scenario, you will create a PowerPoint template, set up a brand color theme with the brand's colors, and add the logo provided.	
2	Step 1: Create the template 1. Open a blank presentation. 2. Choose the page orientation and dimensions you want. 3. Create a **Slide Master**. 4. Save it as a **PowerPoint Template**. Step 2: Set up your custom color theme 1. Customize your colors. 2. Name your custom color theme. 3. Save your custom color theme. Step 3: Add your logo as an image to each header slide	[Provide learners with the problem scenario here.] [Provide learners with the information they need to complete the application (page orientation and dimensions, brand colors, and logo) here.] [Provide learners with the project file, an interactive PowerPoint presentation without graphics or animations here.]

End of the Line

Application for Problem Scenario 6 with No Guidance	
3	If your Powerpoint does not look like the sample provided, you may want to try again or rewatch the demonstration.	[Final PowerPoint with graphics and animations completed correctly is shown here.]

Now, it's your turn! Using the following checklist, create an application with no guidance for problems 6-8 for your course blueprint.

CHECKLIST:

- ☐ Consider the skills you want your learners to practice in problems 6-8
- ☐ Reviewing chapter 7, script out your application for problem scenarios 6-8.
    - Did you use a conversational tone?
    - Did you use second-person pronouns (e.g., you, your, yours)?
    - Did you pitch your script at an 8th grade level?

THE DO IT MESSY APPROACH

End of the Line

Student Examples

Example 1: Applications for Problems 6-8, With No Guidance: Verifying Income

Slide x: Application-Verifying Income and Documenting[30]	
Text	
Text box 1: Now it is your turn to try the income verification process all on your own.	
Text box 2: Here is the situation: You receive only one paystub in Docuware for a customer. They are paid biweekly so you should have received two. The paystub is very recent (June 3, 2022 and the YTD gross is $15,358.45) and you can see that they have likely been employed the full year. You check the notes in CRM and see that this customer is applying for the customer assistance program. Can you use the Year-to-Date method to verify this income? If yes, then how would you calculate it?	
Enter your answer below:	
(Text answer will be input by learner and evaluated by trainer)	
Andrea Speech Bubble: How did you do? Do you feel confident that you tackled that income verification correctly?	
Option 1: Yes, I've got this!	
Option 2: I am not certain I did it correctly, but I feel like I used my resources and did my best.	
Option 3: No, I have no idea what I am doing. I need help.	
Visuals	**Navigation/Animation**
Text box 1	Andrea's speech bubble and the options appear when the learner clicks "Submit" on text box
Speech Bubble	
3 icons with choices	Continue button appears after the learner makes a choice from Andrea's questions.
No guidance or feedback	Previous button to go to previous slide.

---

30 Created by IDOL Colleen Priester.

THE DO IT MESSY APPROACH

Example 2: Applications for Problems 6-8, With No Guidance: Accurately Booking Appointments Application:[31]

Now it's your turn.

Look at these scenarios. Determine if the employee places the appointments in the correct block on the schedule.

Scenario 1 – new patient/wisdom teeth consult

DEE: Good morning, Florida Dental, this is Dee, how may I help you?

PATIENT: Yes, this is Debra Black, I'd like to make an appointment with Dr. Davis because I need my wisdom teeth out. I've never been to your office before.

DEE: Okay Debra, I'd be happy to schedule you for that. This first appointment will be 45 minutes. It includes 15 minutes for x-rays and then 30 minutes with Dr. Davis to speak with you and perform a brief exam. At the end of your consultation, the doctor's assistant will plan with you to schedule your extraction.

I have tomorrow at 7:15 a.m. available for this consultation, would that work for you?

PATIENT: Sounds great, thanks so much.

DEE: My pleasure. I'll put you down for 7:15 a.m. tomorrow and if you could arrive 15 minutes early to fill out paperwork, we would sure appreciate it. If you have dental insurance, go ahead, and bring your card and we'll take a copy of that as well.
PATIENT: Will do, see you tomorrow!

---

31 Created by IDOL Jamie Black.

DEE: Have a great day, Debra.

**Dee adds new patient Debra to a 45-minute "3rds consult" slot in the schedule at 7:15 a.m.*

Is this correct?

[Learner writes and submits their answer]

[Feedback] *YES! Referring to the schedule block image, we can see that 3rds consults are always in the mornings and are 45 minutes in length.*

Scenario 2- established patient/ wisdom teeth extraction

DEE: Good morning, Florida Dental, this is Dee, how may I help you?

PATIENT: Yes, this is John Kruse, I'd like to make an appointment with Dr. Davis for my wisdom teeth extraction. I was there last week for my consultation, but I never made the appointment for the actual surgery.

DEE: Okay John, I'd be happy to schedule you for that procedure. As you know you will be here for one hour. As Dr. Davis and his assistant discussed with you at your consultation, please bring an escort with you, okay? You should have the directions that Dr. Davis gave you last week, so follow those. They can also be found on our website. No food or drink 12 hours before your appointment or we won't be able to do your surgery.

THE DO IT MESSY APPROACH

Okay John I have an opening Tuesday at 7 a.m. Would that work for you?

PATIENT: Yes, thank you!

DEE: My pleasure. I'll put you down for 7 a.m. tomorrow and this will be a one-hour procedure with the doctor.

PATIENT: Will do, see you tomorrow!

DEE: Have a great day, John.

Dee adds John to a 1-hour "3rds Extract" slot in the schedule at 7 a.m. Is this correct?

[Learner writes and submits their answer]

[Feedback] *YES! Referring to the schedule block image we can see that 3rds extract are always in the mornings and are 60 minutes in length.*

Scenario 3- New patient- emergency

DEE: Good morning, Florida Dental, this is Dee, how may I help you?

PATIENT: Yes, my name is Tim Framer and my son, Jonathan just fell off his skateboard and his front tooth is broken, and he says his jaw hurts. My general dentist told me to call you to have him seen by an oral surgeon.

DEE: Okay Tim. We can help you out today. Dr. Davis is booked throughout the day, but I do have slots for emergencies such as

End of the Line

this. You may have a short wait, but we'll get the doctor to see Jonathan as soon as possible between patients, ok? Why don't you head over to our office, and we'll take care of the paperwork and insurance here when you arrive.

PATIENT: Thanks so much, we'll be right there!

Dee adds Tim's son Jonathan to the emergency work-ins slot. Is this correct?

[Learner writes and submits their answer]

[Feedback] *YES! Not only did Dee correctly place Tim's son in the work-in time slot, but she also informed him of their policy on work-ins and that they may have a short wait. This way, Tim isn't upset that he and his son are waiting in the lobby once they arrive.*

Scenario 4- 3rds post-Op

DEE: Good morning, Florida Dental, this is Dee, how may I help you?

PATIENT: Yes, my name is Terry Stewart, and I had my wisdom teeth out last week, I need to be seen again because it feels swollen on my right side. I need to come in today at 3 p.m.

DEE: Okay Terry. You can come in at 3 p.m.

Dee will now add Terry to the 3 p.m. slot for a 3rds post-op. Is this correct?
[Learner writes and submits their answer]

THE DO IT MESSY APPROACH

[Feedback] *NO! - According to the schedule block image, 3rds post-op appointments should only be scheduled from 11 to 12. Here's what Dee could have done instead.*

DEE: Good morning, Florida Dental, this is Dee, how may I help you?

PATIENT: Yes, my name is Terry Stewart, and I had my wisdom teeth out last week, I need to be seen again because it feels swollen on my right side. I need to come in today at 3 p.m.

DEE: Oh Terry, I'm so sorry to hear about the swelling. Dr. Davis reserves post-op appointments from 11 to 12 each day. I do have an opening at 12 today and you would be seen as quickly as possible. If that is not convenient, I can speak with my manager to see if we can put you in at 3 p.m. You would be considered a work-in patient at that time and may have a lengthy wait unfortunately. What would you prefer?

PATIENT: Well, I guess I can get off work early, I'd like to not have to wait. So, yeah, put me in at 12. Thanks

DEE: My pleasure, we'll see you at 12 Terry. Thanks so much!

Is this correct?

[Learner writes and submits their answer]

[Feedback] *In this instance, Dee referred to Florida Dentals schedule block template that has 3rds post-ops from 11-12, but also remembered that she has the option to speak with her manager if the patient is persistent. She also was correct in informing the patient of the lengthy wait they could have experienced if they had chosen to attempt to be seen later in* *the day. This enabled the patient to see the pros and cons of the appointment time and in the end, it was to the patient's benefit (not having to wait) that they came in at Florida Dentals pre-blocked scheduled time for post-ops.*

CHAPTER 13

Hide & Seek

Identify the Component Skills

NOW THAT YOU HAVE SCRIPTED out all of your demonstrations, and applications (phew!), you want to ensure you've included all of the necessary component skills to enable your learners to solve the big problem you started with. Additionally, you want to make sure you have given your learners adequate opportunities to practice each of those component skills.

Component skills are the third ripple in Merrill's Pebble-in-the-Pond model of instruction. After you introduce the big problem and develop your progression of problem scenarios using demonstrations and applications, it's time to make sure your component skills are well represented. At this point, you

THE DO IT MESSY APPROACH

may decide that you want to tweak your problem scenarios to include additional skills or to make the skills you're teaching clearer to your learners. You may also decide you need to add or replace some of your demonstrations or applications. Be open to these possibilities and be willing to be flexible here.

Following Merrill's logic, the reason I direct you to create the problem scenarios and script out the other parts of your course blueprint before coming back to the skills is because I want you to stay focused on the problem-centered aspects of your course. This is the most practical way for learners to understand how to solve a problem. If you instead start with a list of component skills with instructions for your learners to memorize those skills, you risk creating a course blueprint that is overly academic or too technical. The entire point of developing your course using *The Do It Messy Approach* is so that your learners develop the skills they need and are able to put them to work immediately, rather than merely gaining "book knowledge." Remember, we're focused on creating experiential learning here.

That said, now it is time to get a bit technical.

What are component skills?

> **TIP**
>
> Component skills are the steps and conditions required to solve a complex problem or do a complex task.

You likely have included many component skills in your progression of problem scenarios already. Now it's time to identify those component skills and ensure that you have included solid instruction for each one. One advantage of designing your course to take learners through a progression of problems is that component skills required to solve earlier problem scenarios are required for subsequent problems. So one strategy is to demonstrate the skill the first time and then provide an application for the skill later in the course.

> **💡 TIP**
>
> Here, it may be helpful to create a chart for all of the skills you want to teach and to determine when each skill is first introduced in your course blueprint. Make sure the first instance of the component skill is shown in a demonstration. Then when the skill is required for a second use, check to see that it appears in an application.

Here's a chart mapping out one component skill being taught in Step 1 of the Green Possum, Inc. course. As you can see, the first component skill needed to start a sales pitch is understanding the problem your prospect wants to solve. The "tell" column represents when you introduce the concept of starting with the problem. The "show" column represents when you demonstrate how to start with the problem. And the "do" column represents when you ask your learners to apply the skill. Finally, the "guidance" column represents whether or not the application includes guidance:

THE DO IT MESSY APPROACH

Step 1: Starting Your Pitch				
Component Skill #1 = Starting with the Problem				
	Tell	Show	Do	Guidance
Activation and Steps Needed to Solve the Whole Problem	x			
Problem Scenario 1		x		
Problem Scenario 3			x	yes
Problem Scenario 9		x		
Problem Scenario 10			x	no
Real World Application			x	no

Using this chart, we can see that component skill #1: Starting with the Problem, a skill needed to complete Step 1: Starting Your Pitch, appears in five different problem scenarios throughout the course. It appears in two different demonstrations where learners are shown how to use the skill and it appears in three different application scenarios where learners apply the skill themselves, once with guidance and twice without guidance. Now you see how a chart like this can help you create a balanced course that teaches all of the component skills your learners need to know.

In summary, best practices for designing instruction for component skills include the following activities:

- Based on the chart of component skills, design a demonstration for each component skill the first time it is required by a problem.
- Check to be sure that application of the component skill is required by at least two additional problems.

Types of Component Skills

There are three types of component skills corresponding to the three types of generalizable information mentioned previously:

- Concept classification (kinds of)
- Carrying out a procedure (how-to)
- Predicting or visualizing consequences (what happens)

When you think about how to teach someone the skills that fall into these categories, there are two main ways to do so: conveying information or portraying information. Throughout this book, I've encouraged you to concentrate on the portrayal side. Demonstration (show), which Merrill also refers to as "portrayal" is the main way to depict information. However, there may be instances in which you want to simply convey information, when you introduce the steps or skills for the first time, for example. You can also simply convey information when you activate your learners' previous knowledge.

Here is a matrix explaining the types of component skills and which instructional strategies to use:[32]

Table 1. Consistent Information and Portrayal for Categories of Component Skill[‡]

	INFORMATION		PORTRAYAL	
	PRESENT (TELL)	RECALL (ASK)	DEMONSTRATE (SHOW)	APPLY (DO)
Kinds-of	Tell the definition.	Recall the definition.	Show several specific examples.	Classify new examples.
How-to	Tell the steps and their sequence.	Recall the steps and their sequence.	Show the procedure in several different situations.	Carry out the procedure in new situations.
What-happens	Tell the conditions and consequence involved in the process.	Recall the conditions and consequence involved in the process.	Show the process in several different situations.	Predict a consequence or find faulted conditions in new situations.

---

[32] Chapter 3 of First Principles of Instruction: Identifying and Designing Effective, Efficient, and Engaging Instruction.

THE DO IT MESSY APPROACH

Now, it's your turn! Using the following checklist, identify the component skills your course blueprint teaches.

CHECKLIST:

- ☐ Identify the component skills your course covers.
- ☐ Create a chart, like the one in this chapter, mapping out all of the component skills and where each one shows up in the demonstrations and applications you have scripted out. Check to see whether you've adequately taught each one.
- ☐ Make sure each component skill appears at least twice.
    - Once in a demonstration.
    - Once in an application.
- ☐ For bonus points, ensure that for each demonstration, learners are required to practice applying the component skill in at least two additional problem scenarios.

Hide & Seek

THE DO IT MESSY APPROACH

Student Example

Component Skills Chart: Creating a Group in Microsoft Teams

Creating a Teams group[33]				
Component Skill 1 = Being able to create different types of groups, ie staff vs class, depending on needs				
	Tell	Show	Do	Guidance
Activation and Steps Needed to Solve the Whole Problem (video and demonstration)	x	x		
Problem Scenario 1			x	x
Problem Scenario 2			x	x
Problem Scenario 4			x	
Real World Application			x	

Component Skill 2 = Adding members to the group			
	Tell	Show	Do	Guidance
Activation and Steps Needed to Solve the Whole Problem (video and demonstration)	x	x		
Problem Scenario 1			x	x
Problem Scenario 2			x	x
Problem Scenario 4			x	
Real World Application			x	

---

[33] Created by IDOL Rachel Owens.

Component Skill 3 = Choosing an icon or uploading an image for the group				
	Tell	Show	Do	Guidance
Activation and Steps Needed to Solve the Whole Problem (video and demonstration)	x	x		
Problem Scenario 1			x	x
Problem Scenario 2			x	x
Problem Scenario 3			x	x
Problem Scenario 4			x	
Real World Application			x	

CHAPTER 14

Show What You Know

Assessment Design

OKAY, NOW I WANT YOU to put yourself in your client's shoes for a moment. They have hired you to create training for their team. How should they expect to know whether your course is successful? Clearly, you need a procedure for assessing what your learners have gained. Assessment design is a key component of instructional design.

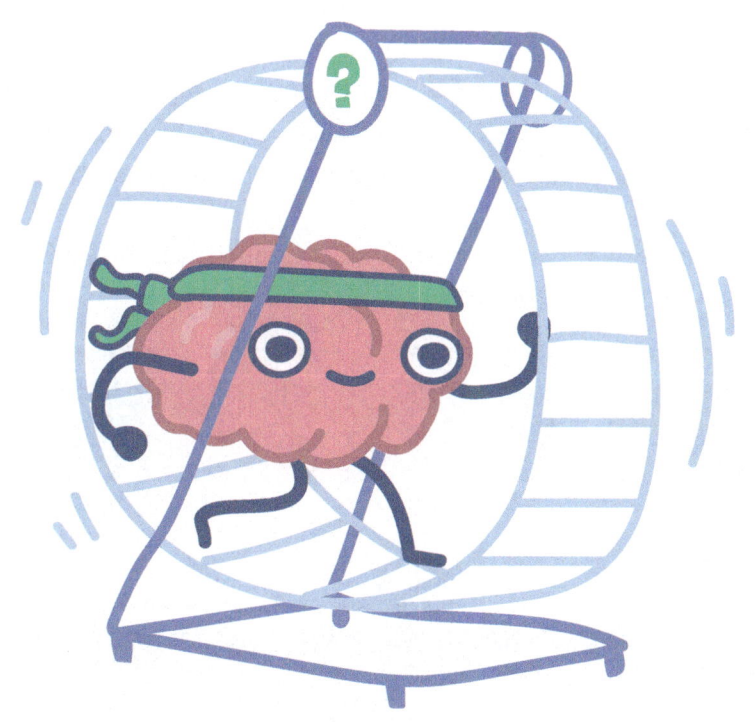

THE DO IT MESSY APPROACH

When it comes to assessing how well your learners can solve the whole problem and apply the component skills you're teaching, there are several methods you could use. At IDOL courses Academy^{SM}, we like to refer to this as the Galaxy of Assessment.

How do you feel about your ability to determine and develop effective assessment strategies?

If you've just created your first course blueprint ever, the truth is that you may not feel all that confident here. But even if you've designed hundreds of courses, the odds are pretty good that you haven't studied effective assessment strategies. So let's talk about it.

First, it's important for you to create assessments that provide meaningful data about the degree to which a learner can perform a task so that your learners (and their supervisors) can further their learning. This means all of your performance goals or outcomes should be based on measurable, observable tasks.

Remember back in Chapter 5, we introduced the ABCD formula for performance goals:

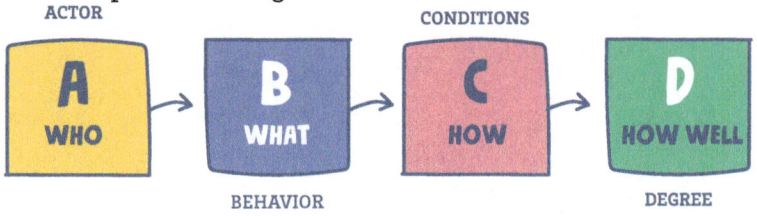

ACTOR	BEHAVIOR	CONDITIONS	DEGREE
A WHO	**B** WHAT	**C** HOW	**D** HOW WELL

- Audience: Who will achieve the objective?
- Behavior: What observable behavior shows mastery of the objective?

- Condition: Under what conditions should they be able to perform the behavior?
- Degree: Are there additional criteria for acceptable performance (e.g., speed, accuracy, quality)?

If the performance goals you have in mind for your learners follow this formula, then designing the proper assessment should be relatively easy. You simply need to ask yourself what you need to observe in your learners to know that they can solve the problem you introduced at the beginning of your course.

ASSESSMENT IS NOT SYNONYMOUS WITH MULTIPLE CHOICE

Most educators use standard multiple choice to assess their learners' skills, when this actually offers the least insight into a learners' mastery of the content. Why is standard multiple choice not the most effective method of assessment? Well, standard multiple choice with (a) - (e) of one-word or very simple answer choices is a passive form of learning. In addition, multiple choice assessments only measure whether a learner is able to remember what they were told. Think back to your own educational experience with multiple choice tests. Now ask yourself, does multiple choice provide meaningful data about the degree to which a learner can perform a task? Not in most cases, I would argue.

Take for example, the Green Possum, Inc. course about crafting a sales pitch. We could take each of the four steps presented and create multiple choice questions to assess how well our learners understand the steps. This data may indicate how well learners remembered (or correctly guessed) specific pieces of information, but it does not demonstrate whether learners can create and deliver a successful sales pitch.

The purpose of assessment is to prove to you, your stakeholders, and your learners that they can solve the problem in front of them. Because multiple choice usually measures low-level thinking and remembering, you can't be sure they can solve the problem on the basis of a multiple choice test. Instead, learners need active forms of learning. This means that your scenarios should make your learners think.

For example, scenarios calling for long-form answers or even multiple choice answers that require serious thinking and attention to detail will ensure that your learners are seeing the nuances in the scenarios you're sharing with them. Observant readers will recall that the earlier applications in the Green Possum course do include questions with multiple choice answers, but those are complex answers that require learners to think and apply the steps they have learned.

In reality, there is a whole galaxy of possible assessment tools to use, including:[34]

- Surveys
- Quizzes
- Scenarios
- Demonstrations
- Reflections
- Simulations
- Games
- Portfolios
- Creations

---

[34] https://www.yourinstructionaldesigner.com/idolgalaxylist

Suppose again for the Green Possum, Inc. course our performance goal is: Within 8 weeks, learners will be able to create a sales pitch for big box representatives with a closing rate of 80%. What would we need to observe in our learners to know that they could do this?

Well, for starters, we would need to observe our learners applying the component skills in each of the four steps (starting your pitch, painting a picture, solving the buyers' problem, and responding to objections) that our course takes them through. We'd also need to see them putting all of the steps together to script out their own sales pitch. Finally, it would help for learners to role play a live sales pitch. Notice how the course asks learners to do each of these tasks.

But of course assessment is only effective when it offers learners the opportunity to improve their performance.

And this is where feedback fits in...

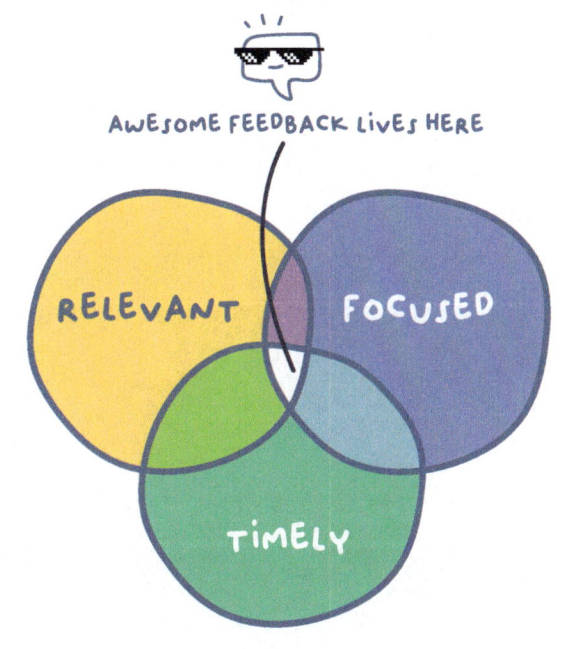

AWESOME FEEDBACK LIVES HERE

RELEVANT   FOCUSED

TIMELY

225

Feedback can be delivered in many ways, but what is essential is that the feedback learners receive is relevant, focused, and timely. Toward the end of the Green Possum, Inc. course, learners are invited to start their own sales pitch. After they do some writing on their own, having been prompted to use the steps they have seen throughout the course, they submit their answers and can then see an example of an "ideal" pitch to which they can compare their own answer. This type of feedback is relevant, focused, and timely – indeed, it's immediate feedback.

> **TIP**
>
> In sum, then, to have an effective assessment, you need to do three things:
> 1. Identify which observable behaviors let you know that your learners can solve the big problem you're teaching them to solve.
> 2. Create **contexts** in which these elements can be demonstrated and applied (these are the problem scenarios you created for your course blueprint).
> 3. Deliver performance **feedback** that describes the degree to which your learners have been successful.

Let me ask you once again: How do you feel about your ability to determine and develop effective assessment strategies? More confident, I hope!

Show What You Know

Now, it's your turn! Using the following checklist, consider what assessment strategies and tools could improve your course blueprint and help your learners master the content.

CHECKLIST:

- ☐ Consider the above galaxy of possible assessment tools. Choose 2-3 you'd like to add to your course.
- ☐ For each assessment, consider where and how you would add it to your course.
- ☐ Script out an assessment for each of your application problem scenarios and add it to your course.
    - Hint: Chapter 18 includes a list of tools you can use to create many of the types of assessments on the list.

CHAPTER 15

Check & Double-Check
Review Each Problem Set

ALTHOUGH YOU HAVE CREATED ALL the different parts of your course in a logical (albeit non-linear) order, the order in which you have created your scenarios is not the order of presentation. You have probably picked up on this already. But I want to make sure there's no confusion about where to place each of the components you've created. Your next step is to put your problem scenarios in the proper order.

THE DO IT MESSY APPROACH

Here is the outline of your course blueprint in the proper order of presentation:

1. Introduction / setting the scene/ activation – stimulate recall and create a structural framework
2. Presentation of the whole problem or whole task – call out the steps along the way
3. Demonstration for problem scenarios 1-2
4. Application with guidance for problem scenarios 3-5
5. Application with no guidance for problem scenarios 6-8
6. Final Demonstration
7. Final Application with no guidance
8. Closing

Here is the complete blueprint of the Green Possum course, designed following the Do It Messy Approach and steps offered in Chapters 5-15:

Slide 1: Title/Intro	
Text Title: How to deliver a sales pitch to big box retailers	
Visuals Image of big box store in the background. Title over background image.	**Navigation/Animation** Image appears first, then the title moves across the screen on a colored bar. Start button appears and advances to next slide.
Slide 2: Setting the Scene	
Text Text box 1: Congratulations! You just landed a new sales position. You've been hired to sell Green Possum, Inc. products to wholesale reps at big box stores. Text box 2: Although you have sales experience, you're a little nervous because you've never pitched big box wholesalers. Text box 3: You know your sales target as a team is to increase sales by 10% this year and you want to do your part to help meet that goal. But there's a lot to learn and you're not sure where to start. Text box 4: What's a new salesperson to do?	
Visuals Text boxes fade in and out over the office background.	**Navigation/Animation** Next and back buttons to advance/repeat text boxes. Continue button at end to go to the next slide.

THE DO IT MESSY APPROACH

Slide 3: Introducing the Whole Shebang
Text Text box 1: Luckily, you have Nicole! Text box 2: Nicole has been the manager of sales at Green Possum, Inc. for five years. You (and everyone else) admire her sales record. If anyone can close a sale, she can. Text box 3: Nicole has agreed to mentor you as you practice your pitch and learn the ropes in your new sales role. Text box 4: If you need help during this training, click on Nicole's icon. She'll have some advice for you.

Visuals	Navigation/Animation
Office background. Nicole character illustration in foreground. Text boxes fade in and out over the office background. Nicole icon appears with text box 4, upper right with arrow (or Nicole pointing?)	Next and back buttons to advance/repeat text boxes. Previous button to go to previous slide. Continue button appears at the end of text boxes to go to the next slide.

Slide 4: Activation and Steps Needed to Solve the Whole Shebang
Text A sales pitch is a condensed version of a sales presentation. Ideally, in less than two minutes, you will explain how Green Possum, Inc.'s green cleaning products work, how they solve your rep's pain points, and the benefits they bring to big box customers. Your pitch should end with an invitation to a longer conversation where you can respond to objections and discuss more details. Before you get started, click on the icons to learn Nicole's approach to pitching big box stores. Icon 1: **Step 1: How to start your pitch.** Starting a pitch is the hardest part. You have to hook your prospect, so they will actually hear the value of the product and how it will benefit their business. When starting your pitch, you will want to integrate the following: start with the problem, personalize the pitch, and mention the stakes.

Slide 4: Activation and Steps Needed to Solve the Whole Shebang
Icon 2: **Step 2: Paint the picture.** Big retailers want to know one thing: How will putting your product on our shelves make us more money or make our customers happier? Give your listeners perspective on who will be buying your product. They want to know that you have a lucrative, robust market of engaged buyers in mind. Icon 3: **Step 3: Explain how the product solves their problem.** Here's where you bring the pitch home. You've explained why you're selling your product and established to whom you're selling. Now you need to establish why they should buy from you. Why is Green Possum, Inc. better than the competition? What is your unique selling proposition? Icon 4: **Step 4: Respond to objections.** In a sales meeting, there are a lot of things which you can't control, but preparing for objections is one thing you absolutely can control. To prepare for objections, anticipate and proactively address concerns up front. When you acknowledge the objection and empathize with your rep, ask clarifying questions, offer a well-positioned rebuttal, and check for feedback, you are doing your best to successfully respond to objections.

Visuals	**Navigation/Animation**
Nicole to the side. Icons and text boxes.	Icons visible. Text boxes associated with each icon appear on each click. Previous button to go to previous slide. Continue button appears after all icons have been clicked to go to the next slide.

THE DO IT MESSY APPROACH

Slide 5: Demonstration – Step 1: Starting Your Pitch (Scenario 1)	
Text: Let's watch Nicole in action. Here she is starting a sales pitch for a rep named Mac from big box store, Wild Earth: **Nicole:** Mac, it's so nice to finally meet you in person. Now I know that in the past you've fielded some customer complaints about green cleaning products not working well or smelling as great as traditional cleaning products. And in our research we've found these are the top two things customers care about when it comes to green cleaning products. Well, not only did Green Possum, Inc. win the Clean Plate Club award for our dishwashing detergent against traditional brands proving how well our product cleans, but we also have a patented scent that people in our focus groups prefer to other brands. [Nicole hands over the open bottle for Mac to smell] What do you think?	
Visuals Create a "pop-up video" style box to show how Nicole's pitch contains the elements mentioned in step 1. Nicole integrated the following: she starts with the problem, personalizes the pitch, and mentions the stakes.	**Navigation/Animation**

234

> **Slide 6: Demonstration – Step 2: Painting the Picture (Scenario 2)**
>
> **Text:**
> Now let's watch what happens as Nicole continues her conversation with Mac.
>
> **Mac:**
> It smells great, Nicole. But... how will putting your product on our shelves make us more money or make our customers happier?
>
> **Nicole:**
> That's a great question! I know, for example, many of the customers who shop at Wild Earth are new moms. New moms love that our products are versatile. You can use the dishwashing detergent as hand soap. You can even use the dishwashing detergent to wash baby clothes. Since it's all natural, it's great for sensitive skin.
>
> [As she speaks, Nicole demos Green Possum products.] And I should know because I happen to be a new mom. Imagine that I'm at home and my baby just woke up from her nap. I need to wash my hands, but all I can find at the moment is Green Possum's dishwashing detergent. No problem! I wash my hands with the dishwashing soap and am ready to comfort the baby.
>
> **Mac:**
> Hmm. That is an interesting selling point. We could even put your product in several different categories on our shelves.
>
> **Nicole:**
> Awesome! I'm sure you know that new moms are one of the fastest growing demographics when it comes to buying green cleaning products. There's something about having new ones at home that makes us super sensitive to smells and chemicals.

THE DO IT MESSY APPROACH

Slide 6: Demonstration – Step 2: Painting the Picture (Scenario 2)	
Visuals Create a "pop-up video" style box to show how Nicole's pitch contains the elements mentioned in step 2. Nicole provides Mac with perspective on who will be buying their product. She lets Mac know that there is a lucrative, robust market of engaged buyers ready to buy.	**Navigation/Animation**
Visuals Text box on office background	**Navigation/Animation** Previous button to go to previous slide. Continue button to advance to the next slide.

Slide 7: Application – Step 1: Starting Your Pitch (Scenario 3)
Text Text box 1: Now it's your turn to practice starting a sales pitch. Suppose you know that Mac's customers have been requesting green cleaning products with refillable options. How would you incorporate this into your pitch? Mac, it's so nice to finally meet you in person. Now I know that some of your customers have been requesting refillable options [complete the pitch by choosing the correct option]. Option 1 [correct]: Did you know that Green Possum, Inc. is testing refill stations at a few stores? Our research shows that the popularity of refill options is growing among younger buyers (e.g., Millennials and Gen Zers) and I know one of your goals is to attract younger buyers. We would be happy to make Wild Earth one of our test stores. What do you think?

> **Slide 7: Application – Step 1: Starting Your Pitch (Scenario 3)**
>
> Option 2: Did you know that Green Possum, Inc. is testing refill stations at a few stores? After we do a test run of say 2 weeks, then we can expand and add refill stations to all of your stores. Our focus group customers really love the refill option. What do you think?
>
> Option 3: Did you know that Green Possum, Inc. is testing refill stations at a few stores? The refill options are self-serve, so you wouldn't need any extra staff to help customers. We would be happy to make Wild Earth one of our test stores. What do you think?
>
> **[Feedback]**
> Option 1: Correct! You started your pitch off well. You started with the problem, personalized the pitch, and mentioned the stakes.
>
> Option 2: You talked about the process and mentioned that focus group customers love the refill option, but what about Wild Earth's customers? You didn't personalize your pitch. Try again.
>
> Option 3: You didn't refer specifically to Wild Earth's customers and why they might want the Green Possum refill option. You didn't personalize your pitch and you jumped straight into an objection which should be raised later in the conversation, if at all. Try again.
>
> **[Advice from Nicole]**
> **Step 1:** Remember, you have to hook your prospect, so they will actually hear the value of the product and how it will benefit their business. When starting your pitch, you will want to integrate the following: start with the problem, personalize the pitch, and mention the stakes.
>
> | **Visuals** | **Navigation/Animation** |
> |---|---|
> | Text box with three choices. | Nicole advice appears on icon click. |
> | Feedback appears after each choice. | Feedback appears depending on which choice is clicked. |
> | | Learner can click multiple times. |
> | **Guidance:** Advice from Nicole shows up with each option to remind learners of step 1. Maybe a "pop-up video" style box appears with each. | Continue button appears after the learner has clicked the correct option. Previous button to go to previous slide. |

THE DO IT MESSY APPROACH

Slide 8: Application – Step 2: Painting the Picture (Scenario 4)

Text
Text box 1: Now it's your turn to practice painting the picture. How would you answer Mac's question: "How will setting up Green Possum, Inc. refill stations make us more money or make our customers happier?"

Option 1: That's a great question! Green Possum, Inc. products are all natural and don't contain any harsh chemicals. Plus, new moms love how versatile our products are. You really shouldn't have any hesitations about letting us set you up with a 2-week trial refill station.

Option 2 [correct]: That's a great question! We know for example that younger buyers want refillable options at a higher rate than other generations, by a 2 to 1 margin, and they are value-based shoppers. In other words, they will shop stores and brands that align with their values. They will also trek across town for buying options that are important to them.

Option 3: That's a great question! Refillable options means less waste in landfills and that should make everyone on the planet happier.

[Feedback]
Option 1: You talked about one set of Wild Earth customers (new moms), but you didn't tie that demographic to the refill option. New moms like the versatility of Green Possum products, but do they want refill options? You haven't answered Mac's question. Try again.

Option 2: Correct! You have given Mac perspective on who will be buying your product and provided details to back up your claims. You have also talked about how engaged the potential market of buyers is.

Option 3: You've talked about one benefit of refillable green products, but you haven't painted a picture for Mac about *his* customers or explained how this option will make his company more money. Try again.

Check & Double-Check

Slide 8: Application – Step 2: Painting the Picture (Scenario 4)		
[Advice from Nicole] **Step 2:** Big retailers want to know one thing: How will putting your product on our shelves make us more money or make our customers happier? Give your listeners perspective on who will be buying your product. They want to know that you have a lucrative, robust market of engaged buyers in mind.		
Visuals	**Navigation/Animation**	
Text box with three choices. Feedback appears after each choice. **Guidance:** Advice from Nicole shows up with each option to remind learners of step 2. Maybe a "pop-up video" style box appears with each.	Nicole advice appears on icon click. Feedback appears depending on which choice is clicked. Learner can click multiple times. Continue button appears after the learner has clicked the correct option. Previous button to go to previous slide.	

Slide 9: Demonstration – Step 3: Explain how the product solves their problem (Scenario 5)
Text Text box 1: Now let's watch Nicole in action once again as she brings her sales pitch home. She explains to Mac why Green Possum, Inc. is better than the competition and puts the benefits of using Green Possum in a broader context. Let's pick up where we left off... **Nicole:** Awesome! I'm sure you know that new moms are one of the fastest growing demographics when it comes to buying green cleaning products. There's something about having new ones at home that makes us super sensitive to smells and chemicals. **Mac:** Oh yeah, I remember how my wife couldn't even go near certain cleaning products after she had our youngest. She only wanted natural products in the house.

239

THE DO IT MESSY APPROACH

Slide 9: Demonstration – Step 3: Explain how the product solves their problem (Scenario 5)
Nicole: Exactly. And I know that your shelves at Wild Earth are full of green product brands. But I'll put the scent of Green Possum products up against any leading green cleaning product on the market. When we tested our product against the competition, not only did we come out on top in terms of cleaning ability, but customers also preferred our fresh scents by a 3 to 1 margin. Also, you should know that we offer retailers a better percentage of sales than anyone in the industry. Not only can you and your customers feel great about your impact on the earth by putting our products on your shelves, but also you can rest assured that by carrying Green Possum products, your profits are rising with every item sold. We even offer a digital display that comes with our refill stations so customers can see the immediate impact they're having by choosing to refill their bottles. We want to partner with all of our retailers in the fight against climate change.

Visuals	**Navigation/Animation**
Create a "pop-up video" style box to show how Nicole's pitch contains the elements mentioned in step 3. Nicole explains to Mac how Green Possum, Inc. is better than the competition and offers a unique selling proposition.	Nicole advice appears on icon click. Feedback appears depending on which choice is clicked. Learner can click multiple times. Continue button appears after the learner has clicked the correct option. Previous button to go to previous slide.

> **Slide 10: Application – Step 3: Explain how the product solves their problem (Scenario 6)**

Text
Text box 1: Now it's your turn. Practice step 3 by considering the following scenarios and choosing the best option for each one.

Customer problem 1: Big box customers are skeptical that green cleaning products work as well as traditional brands, which makes them hesitate to try them. How should you respond?

Option 1: Yes, traditional brands work, that's why they're traditional. But they also work because they include harsh chemicals, which are bad for the environment and sensitive skin.

Option 2: We are happy to supply your store with coupons for Green Possum products, which should entice customers to give them a try. Do your customers like coupons?

Option 3 [correct]: Green Possum, Inc.'s dishwashing detergent has won the Clean Plate award. In a blind test against other green products and traditional brands, Green Possum took home the gold medal and we have special packaging that showcases our award-winning cleaning power.

[Feedback]
Option 1: You don't establish a reason your big box rep should carry your product or how Green Possum solves your customer's problem. Try again.

Option 2: Coupons may be able to solve a problem with the cost of your products. However, the customer problem in this scenario is not about how green products are more expensive than traditional cleaning products. It's about how well they work. Try again.

Option 3: Correct! The Clean Plate club award is a unique selling proposition for Green Possum and it solves your customer's problem.

Customer Problem 2: Environmentally conscious consumers – especially younger shoppers – don't want to buy cleaning products in plastic bottles. They see this as wasteful since a lot of plastic can't be recycled. How should you respond?

THE DO IT MESSY APPROACH

> **Slide 10: Application – Step 3: Explain how the product solves their problem (Scenario 6)**
>
> Option 1: Well, I'm not sure what the alternative might be. Sure, plastics are a problem, but there's really no other way to package some of our products.
>
> Option 2 [correct]: Right, for this reason, we're rolling out refill stations. We're the first in our industry to do so. We believe refill stations would be a great fit for your customers because you have a lot of stores in college towns where research shows there's a high demand for refillable products.
>
> Option 3: While we are rolling out refill stations, we have no immediate plans to go totally plastic free. We find that a lot of our customers are okay with buying plastic bottles as long as they can be recycled.
>
> **[Feedback]**
> Option 1: Even if you can't think of a solution to the problem, you need to give your customer a reason to buy from you. This response makes you seem really inflexible. Try again.
>
> Option 2: Correct! You raise a unique selling proposition for Green Possum that solves your customer's problem. You also explain why it's right for their stores.
>
> Option 3: You offer a partial solution to your customer's problem here in bringing up the refill stations. But you don't talk about it as a unique selling proposition or position it as a solution. Also, you don't respond to the customer's concern about a lot of plastic not being recyclable. Try again.
>
> **[Advice from Nicole]**
> **Step 3: Explain how the product solves their problem.** Here's where you bring the pitch home. You've explained why you're selling your product and established to whom you're selling. Now you need to establish why they'd buy from you. Why is Green Possum, Inc. better than the competition? What is your unique selling proposition?

Slide 10: Application – Step 3: Explain how the product solves their problem (Scenario 6)

Visuals	Navigation/Animation
Text box with three choices. Feedback appears after each choice. **Guidance:** Advice from Nicole shows up with each option to remind learners of step 3. Maybe a "pop-up video" style box appears with each.	Nicole advice appears on icon click. Feedback appears depending on which choice is clicked. Learner can click multiple times. Continue button appears after the learner has clicked the correct option. Previous button to go to previous slide.

Slide 11: Demonstration – Step 4: Respond to Objections (Scenario 7)

Text
Text box 1: Now, let's watch as Nicole handles a series of objections from another big box rep named Mia:

Nicole:
Mia, Green Possum, Inc. offers a completely refillable option. We will supply you with a self-serve refill station where customers can bring back their empty bottles and refill them. All you have to do is call us when you're running low on supply. Our delivery drivers will replenish your refill station at the same time they deliver our other products. Do you want to sign a purchase order?

Mia:
Not yet, Nicole. I have a few more questions. I'm not sure our customers are interested in refillable options. Many of our customers are busy moms who won't remember to bring back empty cleaning bottles to refill.

Slide 11: Demonstration – Step 4: Respond to Objections (Scenario 7)

Nicole:
That's a valid concern, Mia. I'm a busy mom too, so I know how frustrating it is to keep forgetting my refillable bottles at home. Our research shows that interest in refillable cleaning products – even among new moms – is on the rise, though, which is one reason we decided to offer this product line. I also know one of your key KPIs is offering more innovative products. Well, no other green companies in this space offer a full line of refillable cleaning products. Does this answer your question? What other concerns do you have?

Mia:
That is interesting. But we have limited shelf space for green cleaning products. We've been doing business with Mr. Green Jeans for a decade or more and we'd have to stop supplying his products to make room for yours. We've been quite happy with the way his products sell.

Nicole:
Great! I'm not surprised at all that Mr. Green Jeans has kept you happy. I know some of their salespeople and I'm sure they have earned your business. I'm not asking you to give us their shelf space. All I'm asking is if you'll give us a chance to earn your business. What would you say to doing a refill station and a 100-unit test run in a single store?

Mia:
Okay, we can test out the refillable option in our downtown store. A lot of students shop there and may be interested in doing the refillable thing.

Nicole:
Great news! Let's get you set up with a purchasing order for 100 units.

Slide 11: Demonstration – Step 4: Respond to Objections (Scenario 7)	
Visuals	**Navigation/Animation**
Create a "pop-up video" style box to show how Nicole's pitch contains the elements mentioned in step 4. Nicole acknowledges Mia's objection and empathizes with her, asks clarifying questions, offers a well-positioned rebuttal, and checks for feedback.	Nicole advice appears on icon click. Feedback appears depending on which choice is clicked. Learner can click multiple times. Continue button appears after the learner has clicked the correct option. Previous button to go to previous slide.

Slide 12: Application – Step 4: Respond to Objections (Scenario 8)
Text Text box 1: Now it's your turn. Practice step 4 by considering the following scenarios and choosing the best option for each one. Objection 1: Refill stations are messy and hard to use for customers. How should you respond? Option 1 [correct]: These are valid concerns. We have created and tested visual instructions that make our refill stations easy to use. Also we think you'll find our auto shut-off valves to be extremely neat. We can't guarantee there will never be a mess to clean up, but we're continually working to improve this aspect of the refill stations. Does this answer your question? Option 2: You're right, there can be a bit of a learning curve with the refill stations. But we believe that after a few months, your customers won't be able to live without them. Every innovative product faces this kind of challenge. Option 3: You're not giving your customers enough credit. Customers who really appreciate refill stations are willing to go out of their way to use them. We just signed an agreement with your closest competitor. You don't want to be left behind. Do you want to sign a purchase order?

THE DO IT MESSY APPROACH

> **Slide 12: Application - Step 4: Respond to Objections (Scenario 8)**
>
> **[Feedback]**
> Option 1: Correct! You offer a well-positioned rebuttal that addresses the specifics of the objection and check for feedback.
>
> Option 2: You haven't really addressed the objection. The concern is about the immediate issues with a refill station and your response asks your prospect to focus on the long-term instead. This is more of a distraction strategy. Try again.
>
> Option 3: You don't empathize with your listener's concern, instead you question whether their objection is valid. Then you respond with a hard-selling tactic. This is not likely to get you the result you want. Try again.
>
> Objection 2: Refill options make pricing too confusing for customers. How should you respond?
>
> Option 1: Let us worry about pricing. It's not your concern.
>
> Option 2 [correct]: It's true that most refill stations require a scale or some other mechanism for determining the price. But our refill stations have a digital pricing monitor that gives customers a printout they can take to the cash register to scan. It's easy!
>
> Option 3: Stores like yours have been offering bulk food for decades. Why do you think customers will be confused by a soap refill station? This is really the same model as bulk food. Will you give us a chance to prove you wrong?
>
> **[Feedback]**
> Option 1: This response doesn't acknowledge the objection. It's dismissive and doesn't address the core of the listener's concern. Try again.
>
> Option 2: Correct! You acknowledge the objection and offer a clear rebuttal.

Check & Double-Check

Slide 12: Application – Step 4: Respond to Objections (Scenario 8)
Option 3: You challenge the objection here, rather than empathizing with your listener's concern. It's a good idea to tie the refill station to something that you know is working for the customer, but you need to make sure the assumptions you're making are valid. Try again. **[Advice from Nicole]** **Step 4: Respond to objections.** In a sales meeting, there are a lot of things which you can't control, but preparing for objections is one thing you absolutely can control. To prepare for objections, anticipate and proactively address concerns up front. When you acknowledge the objection and empathize with your rep, ask clarifying questions, offer a well-positioned rebuttal, and check for feedback, you are well prepared to overcome objections.

Visuals	Navigation/Animation
Text box with three choices. Feedback appears after each choice. **Guidance:** Advice from Nicole shows up with each option to remind learners of step 4. Maybe a "pop-up video" style box appears with each.	Nicole advice appears on icon click. Feedback appears depending on which choice is clicked. Learner can click multiple times. Continue button appears after the learner has clicked the correct option. Previous button to go to previous slide.

THE DO IT MESSY APPROACH

> **Slide 13: Final Demonstration – Steps 1-4 (Scenario 9)**
>
> **Text:**
> Now, let's watch Nicole in action one more time as she does a full pitch following steps 1-4. Here she is demonstrating a brand new product line for a rep named Kim from big box store, East Coast Naturals:
>
> **Nicole:**
> Kim, it's good to see you again. I'm excited to be able to show you more of Green Possum, Inc.'s best selling products. Customers who care about the environment also care about what they put on their skin. That's why in addition to our cleaning line with refillable options, we've introduced a line of skincare products. Right now, they're only available on our website, but we're thinking of bringing them to retail. I know skincare is one of East Coast Naturals' biggest sellers and you've been on the frontier of safer skincare. Would you consider being our exclusive retail partner for Green Possum skincare?
>
> **Nicole:**
> That's a great question! We're prepared to offer every Green Possum, Inc. customer a free sample of our BPA-free sunscreen. [Hands Kim a sample of the sunscreen.] We'll add the samples to current product packages in our next product distribution run.
>
> We know your biggest customer base is moms with kids under 5 and moms are especially concerned about the dangers of regular sunscreen. And I'm sure you've seen the recent article in *Parenting* magazine about the white-washing of green sunscreen. Many of the allegedly natural brands out there contain ingredients that are banned in most countries outside the U.S. Our sunscreen has been certified as the safest on the market.
>
> So this will be an easy way to get moms' attention and shift their loyalty from our cleaning products over to the skincare line. With summer coming up, we think this will be a big hit. Our marketing team is also putting the finishing touches on a point-of-sale display to draw attention to the new products.

Check & Double-Check

> **Slide 13: Final Demonstration – Steps 1-4 (Scenario 9)**
>
> **Kim:**
> Hmm. We are happy to continue giving you shelf space for your cleaning products, but Health & Beauty is tougher. That area of the store is smaller and we're already running out of space.
>
> **Nicole:**
> I totally understand. There's only so much space in your stores. What if we started with just the sunscreen and you put it in the seasonal section of the store, rather than taking up precious space in Health & Beauty? That would give us a few months to test the product and then make a decision about carrying our other skincare products in the fall.
>
> **Kim:**
> That's a good idea. I've also been meaning to talk to our store designer about expanding Health & Beauty. Those products are always popular with our customers, especially in the Shop Local section.
>
> **Nicole:**
> Good to know. Since all of Green Possum, Inc.'s products are manufactured in our Atlanta, GA facility, we'd love to add our skincare products to the local products section of your Atlanta stores. Do any of those locations have openings for products in Health & Beauty?
>
> **Kim:**
> I'm not sure, but I can put you in touch with our Atlanta rep, Gretchen.
>
> **Nicole:**
> Great! Yes, I'd love to talk with Gretchen. I'll get you set up with the sunscreen samples and a run of 100 units for the seasonal section.
>
> **Advice from Nicole Infographic:**
> **Step 1: How to start your pitch.** Starting a pitch is the hardest part. You have to hook your prospect, so they will actually hear the value of the product and how it will benefit their business. When starting your pitch, you will want to integrate the following: start with the problem, personalize the pitch, and mention the stakes.

THE DO IT MESSY APPROACH

> **Slide 13: Final Demonstration - Steps 1-4 (Scenario 9)**

Step 2: Paint the picture. Big retailers want to know one thing: How will putting your product on our shelves make us more money or make our customers happier? Give your listeners perspective on who will be buying your product. They want to know that you have a lucrative, robust market of engaged buyers in mind.

Step 3: Explain how the product solves their problem. Here's where you bring the pitch home. You've explained why you're selling your product and established to whom you're selling. Now you need to establish why they should buy from you. Why is Green Possum, Inc. better than the competition? What is your unique selling proposition?

Step 4: Respond to objections. In a sales meeting, there are a lot of things which you can't control, but preparing for objections is one thing you absolutely can control. To prepare for objections, anticipate and proactively address concerns up front. When you acknowledge the objection and empathize with your rep, ask clarifying questions, offer a well-positioned rebuttal, and check for feedback, you are doing your best to successfully respond to objections.

Visuals	**Navigation/Animation**
Somehow point out each step in their convo. Maybe a "pop-up video" style box appears with each	

> **Slide 14: Application - Steps 1-4 (Scenario 10)**

Text
Text box 1:
Now it's your turn. Imagine that Nicole has spoken to Gretchen, East Coast Naturals' Atlanta rep, and booked a sales pitch for you. Your job is to pitch Gretchen Green Possum, Inc.'s new skincare line. You know that the "shop local" section of the store is very popular and that's good news because Green Possum is an Atlanta-based company. You also know that Gretchen has been looking for a natural skincare line that will be popular with women over 50.

Nicole speech bubble 1: Read this scenario. How would you start your pitch for Gretchen? After you write your answer, click submit, and compare it to Nicole's sample pitch.

> **Slide 14: Application - Steps 1-4 (Scenario 10)**
>
> Text box 2: [Learner writes.]
>
> Text box 3 [appears after learner has submitted their response]: Nicole's sample pitch: Hi Gretchen! It's great to meet you. I'm excited to show you Green Possum, Inc.'s brand new skincare line made right here in Atlanta. Now, I know that you're looking for a product that will be popular with women over 50. And our products have tested exceptionally well with this demographic. Not only do they appreciate our natural, fresh scents, but they love the way our products moisturize their skin. Given all of our research, I believe your customers will be excited about our products.
>
> Nicole speech bubble 2:
> Is your answer similar to mine? Did you start with the problem, personalize the pitch, and mention the stakes?
>
> Text box 1:
> Now suppose Gretchen asks, "How will putting your product on our shelves make us more money or make our customers happier?"
>
> Nicole speech bubble 1: Read this scenario. How would you paint the picture for Gretchen? After you write your answer, click submit, and compare it to Nicole's example.
> Text box 2: [Learner writes.]
>
> Text box 3 [appears after learner has submitted their response]: Nicole's example: Great question! Our research shows that women over 50 are most concerned with two things when it comes to skincare: Will it make me look younger? And, will it feel good on my skin? The women in our focus group ranked Green Possum's skincare products higher than the competition on both counts. To get the word out about our products, we've created an ad campaign to target this age demographic and we'll include East Coast Naturals under the "where to buy" section. We believe having our products on your shelves will bring in a wave of new customers to East Coast Naturals.
>
> Nicole speech bubble 2:
> Is your answer similar to mine? Did you give Gretchen perspective on your product? Did you show her that you have a lucrative, robust market of engaged buyers in mind?

THE DO IT MESSY APPROACH

> **Slide 14: Application – Steps 1-4 (Scenario 10)**
>
> Text box 1:
> "Okay," says Gretchen. "In the past, when we've tested skincare products in our stores, we've found that if customers can't try the product in the store, they will try it at home and bring it back for a refund if they don't like it. This costs us money."
>
> Nicole speech bubble 1: Read this scenario. How does your product solve Gretchen's problem? After you write your answer, click submit, and compare it to Nicole's example.
>
> Text box 2: [Learner writes.]
>
> Text box 3 [appears after learner has submitted their response]: Nicole's example: Ah yeah, it's really important for customers to be able to try new skincare products in the store. We're happy to provide you with product testers and free samples. Also, unlike our competitors, we will reimburse you for any customer refunds. All you have to do is save the returned products and return them to us. At Green Possum, Inc., we stand behind our products.
> Nicole speech bubble 2:
> Is your answer similar to mine? Did you explain why Green Possum is better than the competition? Did you offer a unique selling proposition?
>
> Text box 1:
> "That's good to know," says Gretchen. "Still, your product retails for about 10% more than our current best selling skincare products. I don't know if our customers will pay more."
>
> Nicole speech bubble 1: Read this scenario. How would you respond to Gretchen's objection? After you write your answer, click submit, and compare it to Nicole's response.
>
> Text box 2: [Learner writes.]

252

Slide 14: Application - Steps 1-4 (Scenario 10)

Text box 3 [appears after learner has submitted their response]:
Nicole's response: Yes, we're sensitive to this concern. We're aware of the price difference and we've priced our products really intentionally. Unlike our competitors who cut corners by adding alcohol or water to their products, we use premium quality aloe or natural oils as a base. Our marketing department is working on packaging that highlights this difference. And if you're willing to work with us on product placement, we believe customers will pay more for a superior product. Does this answer your question?

Nicole speech bubble 2:
Is your answer similar to mine? Did you acknowledge the objection and empathize with Gretchen, ask clarifying questions, offer a well-positioned rebuttal, and check for feedback?

Visuals	Navigation/Animation
Office background with three text boxes—1 top and centered, 2 below one and to the left, 3 aligned with 2 and to the right: | 1 | | 2 | 3 | Nicole appears to the right of 3, gesturing to the answer with a speech bubble. **No Guidance**	1 & 2 always appear. Nicole's speech bubble 1 is visible at first. Text in 3 and Nicole's speech bubble 2 only appear after the learner writes in 2 and clicks "submit." Continue button appears after the learner has clicked Submit. Previous button to go to previous slide.

THE DO IT MESSY APPROACH

Slide 15: Application – Steps 1-4 (Real World Application)	
Text Text box 1: Now it's time for you to take the lessons learned here out into the real world. Write up a sales pitch for one of your own prospects and role play that pitch with one of your colleagues or your manager. Nicole speech bubble 1: Now it's your turn. Can you write a sales pitch? Text box 2: [Learner writes.] Nicole speech bubble 2: Does your pitch include all 4 steps? Nicole speech bubble 3: If you need to review the steps return to the infographic on a previous slide. Now that you have a sales pitch, practice it with one of your colleagues or your manager and ask for critical feedback.	
Visuals Office background with three text boxes—1 top and centered, 2 below one and to the left, 3 aligned with 2 and to the right: ┌─────────────┐ │ 1 │ ├──────┬──────┤ │ 2 │ 3 │ └──────┴──────┘ Nicole appears to the right of 3, gesturing to the answer with a speech bubble. No Guidance	Navigation/Animation 1 & 2 always appear. Nicole's speech bubble 1 is visible at first. Text in 3 and Nicole's speech bubble 2 only appear after the learner writes in 2 and clicks "submit." Continue button appears after the learner has clicked Submit. Previous button to go to previous slide.

Once you have completed your course blueprint and put all of the scenarios in an order that will make sense to your learners, take at least a day or two away from your course to gain a little perspective before coming back to do your final review.

> **💡 TIP**
>
> It's important that you don't skip this step. I'm serious. Even if you're tempted to jump right into reviewing your scenarios, I want you to take a beat because you need fresh eyes to do your final review.

When you're ready to come back and take a look at the whole course, review the progression of scenarios to see whether it still makes sense to you. Then, look at each problem scenario, one-by-one to make sure each one teaches the component skills you identified in the previous chapter. Next, double-check your chart of component skills. Is each component skill adequately addressed throughout the course with one demonstration and at least one application for each skill? Have you adequately activated learners' prior knowledge? Finally, look at the performance goal you identified initially. Will this course blueprint help your learners achieve that performance goal?

Now, it's your turn! Using the following checklist, review each problem set in your course blueprint.

CHECKLIST:

- ☐ Put your problem scenarios into an order that makes logical sense for your learners.
- ☐ Take a day or two off!
- ☐ Review the progression of scenarios. Does it still make sense?
- ☐ Review each problem scenario. Does each one adequately teach the component skills that appear in each scenario?
- ☐ Review your chart of component skills. Do you need to add any more problem scenarios to your course?
- ☐ Have you activated your learners' previous knowledge in the appropriate places?
- ☐ Does this course help learners reach the performance goal you set out to teach?
- ☐ Revisit your needs analysis. Does your course answer all 22 questions to your satisfaction?
- ☐ Revisit your task analysis. Are all of your main and subtasks covered?

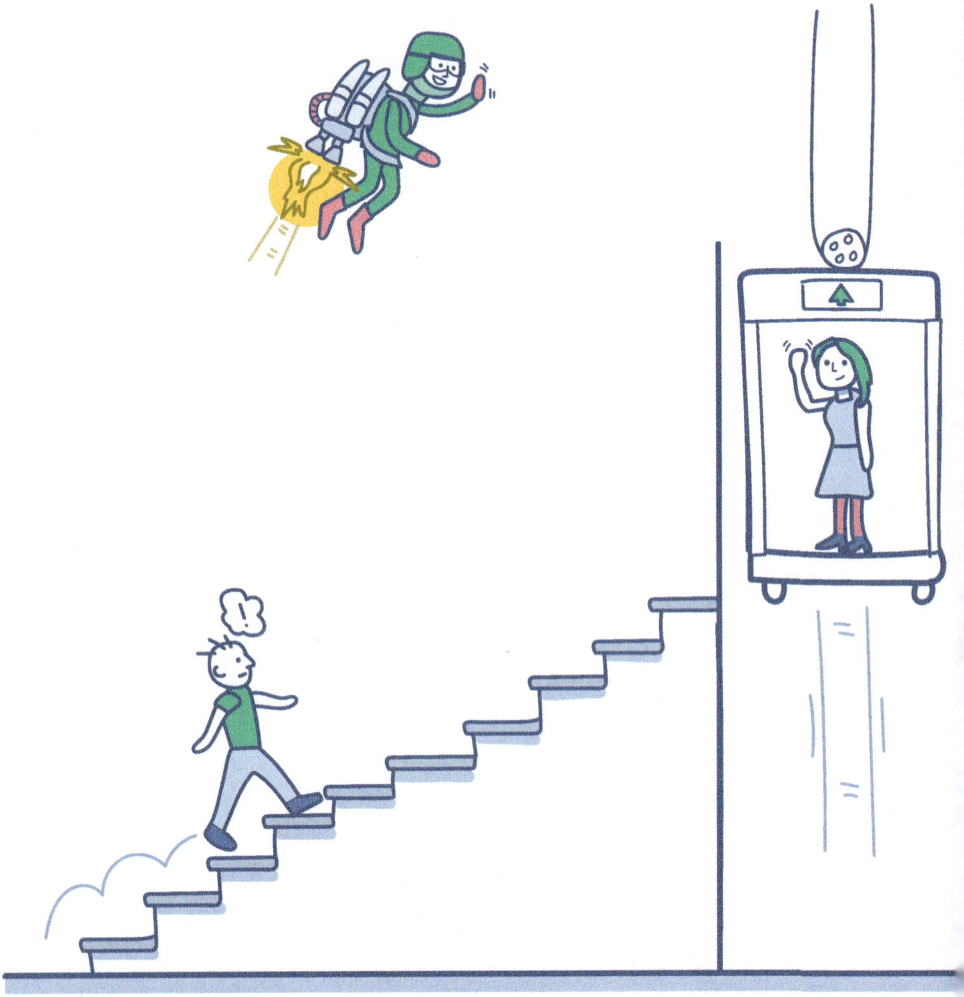

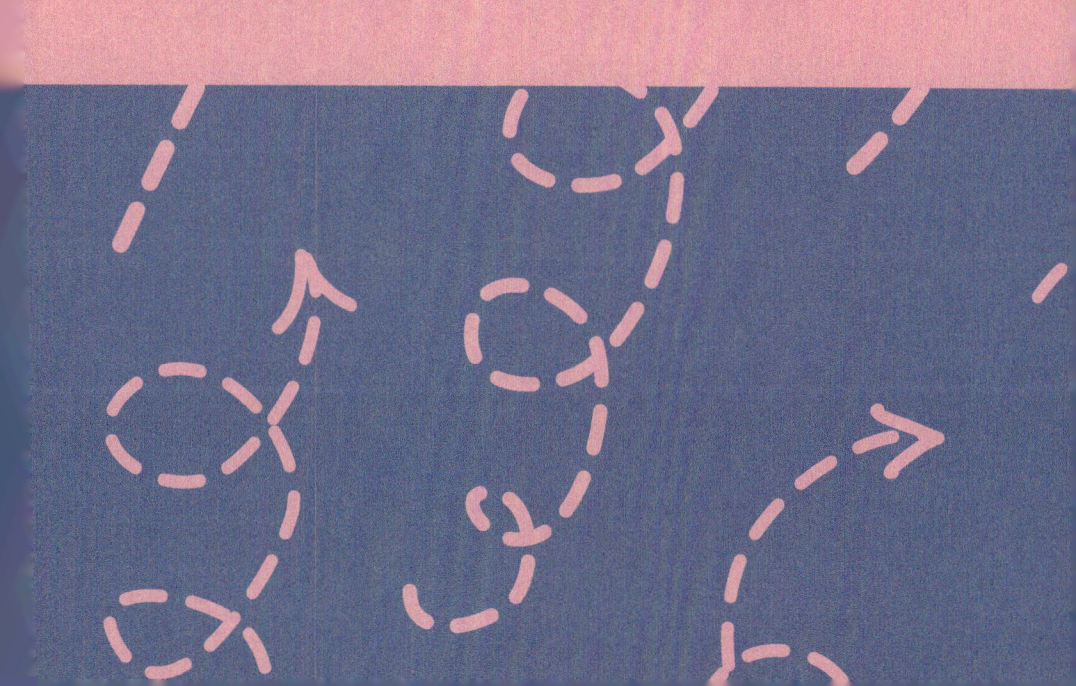

PART THREE
ENHANCEMENT & NEXT STEPS

CHAPTER 16

Integrato Enhanceum

Integration & Enhancement Strategies

OKAY, YOU'VE GOT A COMPLETE course blueprint now. Congratulations! You are a true instructional designer and online learning (IDOL™) developer. You could stop here and begin building your course using Articulate Storyline or whatever other course design technology you want to use (see the list of tools in Chapter 18: Further Research and Resources).

Suppose you want to take your course further, though. Suppose you want to include some ways for your learners to integrate the component skills they learned through your course into their everyday lives. In this chapter, I go over some integration and enhancement strategies you may also want to consider.

To take your course to the next level, consider how you can prompt your learners to continue the process of learning after completing your course. You have already set out to transform your learners from people who could not solve the big problem you started with way back in chapter 5, into those who could solve this problem. And when we transform people, what we're really talking about is changing their brains. So in order to better understand how to make what you've already taught "stickier," let's first look at a brief primer about how human beings learn stuff.

THE COGNITIVE SCIENCE OF LEARNING

Learning isn't all about memory, but memory is certainly one component of learning. So the first question is what is memory? Memory is basically our capacity to store and retrieve information. To form a memory, our brain goes through two processes: encoding and storage. When we acquire information, our brain encodes it so that we can add it to our "file system" and maintain it in either short term or long term memory. From there, when we want to recall the information, we can easily retrieve it from our brain's storage facility. Retrieval is the third process involved here.[35]

You can think of your long term memory as a huge warehouse with nearly unlimited storage space. Your short term memory, on the other hand, is the equivalent of a shoebox and only holds

---

[35] Zlotnik, G. and Vansintjan, A. (2019). "Memory: An Extended Definition," Frontiers in Psychology. https://doi.org/10.3389/fpsyg.2019.02523.

Integrato Enhanceum

enough information to process and manipulate for the purpose of solving particular problems. The Goal of your course and the purpose behind the Do It Messy Approach is to take your learners from remembering they've seen something before to properly mastering that knowledge.

So if mastery is your goal for your learners, you want them not only to apply the component skills you've demonstrated within your course, but also to apply those component skills outside of your course. Think back to the Green Possum, Inc. sales course we've been discussing all along. What's the best learning scenario you can imagine for teaching someone sales skills? Well, putting those skills to work during real-world scenarios of course. This is why that sample course ends with a prompt to script out their own sales pitch and role play it with their manager or a colleague.

CYCLE OF LEARNING

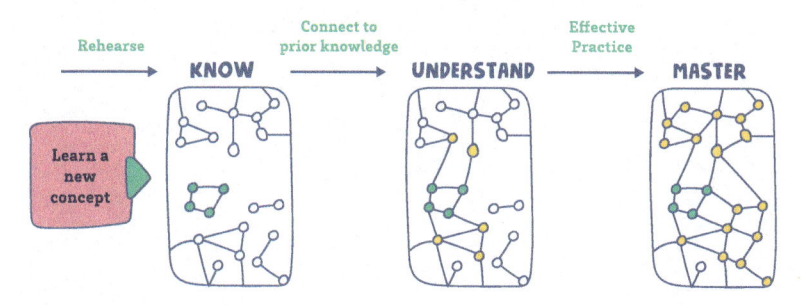

Learn a new concept → **KNOW** — Rehearse → Connect to prior knowledge → **UNDERSTAND** — Effective Practice → **MASTER**

This approach also fits with the cycle of learning. Whenever you teach a new concept, you activate prior knowledge, you demonstrate it, and you ask your learners to apply that concept. Integration takes this cycle one step further. For mastery, your learners must effectively practice the concept in many different scenarios, including in real-world scenarios.

Based on what we know about the science of learning, let's turn to some of the learning strategies you could use to take your course blueprint up a notch.

6 INTEGRATION & ENHANCEMENT LEARNING STRATEGIES[36]

1. Spaced Practice helps your learners continue their mastery of a skill over a long period of time. Spaced practice happens when, rather than cramming for an exam or assessment, you return to a skill that you were taught some time ago. When reviewing content for your learners, make sure you review not only the previous lessons but older content as well. Objectively, there isn't an optimal spacing interval. However, researchers agree that the "sweet spot" is when remembering the content is doable, but effortful, so information can be reconsolidated and strengthened.

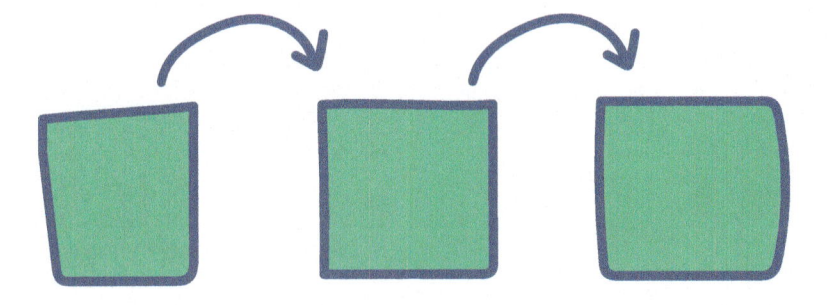

2. Retrieval Practice gives learners the opportunity to go back into their long-term memory to pull out information stored previously. To use retrieval practice, you can ask learners to put away their notes and write down all they can remember

---

36 https://www.cultofpedagogy.com/learning-strategies/

about a topic or process. Then, they should check and complement their answers. It is important that accuracy is checked to avoid misconceptions. An effective idea is to provide them with as many practice scenarios as possible (so you may want to create bonus applications for learners who want more practice, for example). You could also suggest that learners create their own questions and exchange them with colleagues. Frequent low-stake quizzes or practice activities at the beginning of a lesson are highly recommended if it is a topic that takes more than one lesson to master.

3. Elaboration involves asking learners to describe and explain the content in as many details as possible as well as linking it to other content and personal experiences. The advantage of using this technique is that learners create multiple connections between the new piece of information and things they already know, making it easier for the relevant memory traces to be reactivated in the future.

THE DO IT MESSY APPROACH

4. Interleaving is an advanced technique that requires learners to practice switching between problems, topics, or ideas and keeping up with new topics. Instead of practicing a single skill over and over before moving on to the next skill, interleaving blends several related skills in one task. Mixing up problems and questions that demand different solving strategies is also interleaving.

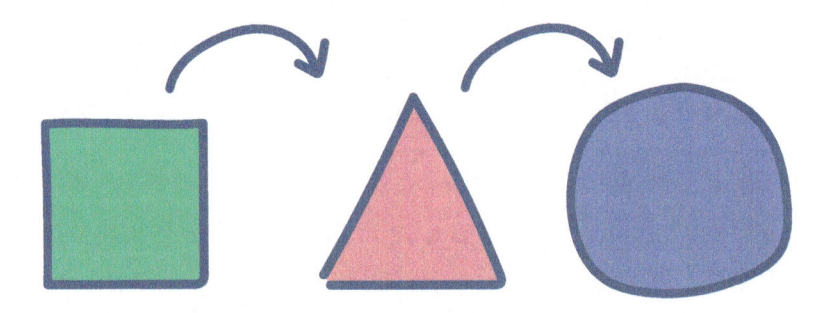

5. Concrete Examples going beyond the problem scenarios you've shared with learners, you may want to add examples that your learners can relate to. When teaching, use as many examples as possible, linking the content to each example. The connection between examples and concepts should be made clear and detailed. If you leave your learners to make their own connections, they may not connect the right dots.

Integrato Enhanceum

6. Dual Coding is the strategy of using different media to teach and learn. For example, the use of diagrams, timelines, infographics, mind maps, and colors helps learners understand concepts and also remember them better. However, be careful not to use too many sources at the same time, as this may considerably increase learners' working memory load, leading to cognitive overload.

Additional resources for each of these strategies appear in chapter 18, so if you want to use any of them to enhance your course, I suggest you start with those resources.

More on Integration

According to research on instruction, M. David Merrill suggests integration activities should provide:[37]

1. Techniques that encourage learners to integrate (transfer) the new knowledge or skill into their everyday life.
2. Opportunity for the learner to publicly demonstrate their new knowledge or skill.

---

37 https://learn.canvas.net/courses/903/pages/integration

3. Opportunity for learners to reflect-on, discuss, and defend their new knowledge or skill.
4. Opportunity for learners to create, invent, or explore new and personal ways to use their new knowledge or skill.

Examples of Integration Instructional Activities

Examples of types of integration phase activities include:
- Ponder activities, which aid your learners to think broadly and deeply about a topic.
- Stories by learners, which encourage your learners to correlate new information with their life.
- Job aids, which help your learners as a reminder to apply their learning to real-life situations.
- Research activities, which encourage your learners to discover and use their own sources of information.

Ponder Activities

Ponder activities prompt your learners to think deeply and broadly about the subject. They encourage your learners to examine their ideas from a new perspective. Types of ponder activities include:
- Question or reflection prompts: Asking your learners rhetorical or reflection questions helps learners to make connections. Making the questions personal will require the learners to think about the subject and their world. Examples of questions can be:
    - Why do you think this is so?
    - Why did this happen?
    - Where will this idea apply?

Integrato Enhanceum

○ Where will it not apply?

○ How important is this idea to you?

○ What other results could you expect?

- Cite example activities: This type of activity requires learners to identify existing examples.

- Evaluations activities: This type of activity requires your learners to critically examine the importance and relevance of items of learning. These activities prepare learners to apply new knowledge by recalling needed information. When using evaluation activities, you may have your learners evaluate real-world examples (e.g., press releases, advertisements, posters, organization charts, book jackets, reviews or synopses) to relate the subject matter to real-world context.

Stories by the Learners

One way to promote the integration of new information into their life is to encourage learners to retrieve events from their own lives or to apply skills they're learning to situations they're experiencing now. You can encourage your learners by sharing your story and asking them to share their stories. The invitation to tell a story adds the element of reflection and encourages learners to think about what is said and how it applies to their own situations.

Job Aids

Job aids are instruction cards or wall charts that allow your learners to access the information they need when performing a task. Job aids can be quite handy when your learners apply new information. They can be used to provide help to someone performing a task right when and where they need it. There are different types of job aids, such as checklists, reference summaries (cheat sheets), glossaries, and calculators.

Research Activities

Research activities require your learners to discover and use their own sources of information. You can use research activities to teach your learners how to gather, analyze, and report on information. Examples of research activities include:

- Personal perspectives: Ask your learners to consider the research of all different perspectives to augment their own.
- Scrapbooks: Ask your learners to create a scrapbook so that they can gather and organize their knowledge.
- Day in the life: Have your learners research a real, historical, or fictional character and then ask them to imagine how the character would use the new information in a typical day.

Now, it's your turn! Using the following checklist, consider what integration and enhancement strategies could improve your course blueprint and help your learners master the content.

CHECKLIST:

- ☐ Consider the above integration & enhancement strategies. Choose 2-3 you'd like to add to your course.
- ☐ For each strategy, consider where and how you would add it to your course.
- ☐ Script out each integration & enhancement strategy and add it to your course.
    - Hint: In chapter 18, there are resources to help you better understand each of the strategies above.

CHAPTER 17

There is No Failure, Only Feedback

Get Feedback

IN CHAPTER 14, WE DISCUSSED assessment and ensuring that your learners get relevant, focused, and timely feedback. Well, it turns out that this is just as important for you and your course blueprint.

You can think of creating a course as similar to producing a movie in Hollywood. There are certain groups of people who need to sign-off on a film at each stage in its development. For example, once a movie script is written, editors need to come

THE DO IT MESSY APPROACH

in and make changes, producers need to approve the final version, and the director needs to "okay" different scenes. Then, once the actors have come in and all the scenes have been shot, editors come in again to cut and splice everything together, sound and special effect technicians do their magic, some scenes will need to be reshot, and once again, producers and the director sign-off on the final edits.

You also need to receive strategic feedback on your course throughout the different stages of production.

There are three main groups from whom you need feedback:

1. SMEs
2. Stakeholders
3. Learners

Subject Matter Experts

You have already talked to your SMEs after completing your quick & dirty needs analysis (Chapter 3) and potentially at the point where you were developing your task analysis (Chapter 4) to ensure that you haven't missed anything that your course should include. Also, after you brainstormed your list of problem scenario briefs (Chapter 8), you checked-in with SMEs to ensure your problem scenarios were realistic and accurate. Now that you have completed the draft content for your course, you should return to your SMEs for feedback once again.

At this point, make sure to ask for specific and actionable feedback. Remind your SMEs that you are asking them to sign-off on the script for your course. It's important to take this step before you spend a lot of time on your visual design.

There is No Failure, Only Feedback

Here, you're asking them to give you feedback on the course content itself. Tell them you'll come back for feedback on the visuals after you have incorporated whatever recommendations they offer for adjusting your script.

From your SMEs, you're looking for feedback around accuracy, flow, and whether you have realistic scenarios. To get specific and constructive feedback, tell your SMEs where you are with your course (i.e., what stage), where you want to be, and what you want them to look for. This will ensure that you get the most actionable and specific feedback. Also, revisit the section called "Tips for Getting Quality Feedback from SMEs" in chapter 4 for help with this part.

Stakeholders

You also want your stakeholders (e.g., clients) to sign off on the script for your course. Here you want to check in to ensure that your stakeholders understand how your course is designed to accomplish the performance goals you all agreed upon before you started building your course. Ideally, stakeholders will sign-off on the performance goal, the full script of your course blueprint, and after you add in your visuals. Again, it's important to get their sign-off on the content itself before you move to working on the visual design.

Learners

Obviously, you won't be able to get feedback from your whole population of learners or potential learners. So you need to find a good sample of learners to offer constructive feedback. Recall that during the quick and dirty needs analysis, I recommended that you interview no more than five employees (a mix of supervisors, high and under performers). Again, I

THE DO IT MESSY APPROACH

recommend that you be strategic about how many learners you ask for feedback here (five is a good number here as well). Also, keep in mind that it may be less helpful to share your script itself with learners. Instead, you may want to sit down with them and walk them through the scenarios, so they (and you) get a sense of what it will be like to take the course.

With learners, you'll mainly be looking for feedback on comprehension, rather than on accuracy. For an eLearning course, once you have created the script and a visual design, usually a prototype, it will be helpful to sit down with your learners and watch them interact with your design. Do they follow the course in the way you intend? Are the instructions for assessments clear and complete? Is the course easy to use? Make sure to get specific and actionable feedback from your learners.

Now, it's your turn! Using the following checklist, get feedback from stakeholders, subject matter experts, and learners.

CHECKLIST:

- ☐ Share your course blueprint with SMEs for feedback.
- ☐ Share your course blueprint with stakeholders for feedback.
- ☐ Share your course blueprint with a sample set of learners (e.g., 5) for feedback.

There is No Failure, Only Feedback

- ☐ Ask for specific and actionable feedback from each of your groups.
- ☐ Analyze the feedback.
- ☐ Come up with a plan for incorporating feedback.
- ☐ Incorporate the feedback.
- ☐ Return to each group to ensure you've integrated their feedback well.
- ☐ Repeat for each stage in your course development.

CHAPTER 18

Further Research and Resources

YOU CAN FIND AN ELECTRONIC version of this resources list on www.idolcourses.com/doitmessy

I've been an instructional designer and online learning developer since 2012. The best part of being an IDOL is the continuous learning and growth that is both a requirement and outcome of being an instructional designer. Enjoy your journey to become an IDOL and save time by using these resources to learn more about this field and our practice.

Disclosure: Some of the links below are affiliate links, which means if you use these links to make a purchase, I will get a

small commission at no additional cost to you. You can choose not to use them if you'd like — the decision is yours; either way, these tools are great! See the full disclosure here.

Getting Started with Instructional Design

When you're getting started, it's hard to figure out what you should focus on. Each of these resources is about how to get started and where to begin your journey to become an IDOL™.

IDOL™ courses Blog: The IDOL™ courses blog is written by IDOL courses Academy^{SM} alumni. They share their best tips, advice, and practical steps to help you on your journey to becoming an IDOL™.

Land Your First IDOL™ Job: Masterclass Replay: Watch and access the free training on how to prepare for your first IDOL™ job. This training was created and delivered by me, Dr. Robin Sargent, owner, and founder of IDOL™ courses.

Become an IDOL™: Getting Started Challenge: This is a free 5-day training and challenge that opens just four times a year. You'll learn corporate instructional design principles and how we select development tools so you can create several pieces for your portfolio with just one course topic.

Become an IDOL™ Facebook Group: Join our free IDOL™ community to get feedback, answers for your questions, network with others, and find more resources.

Become an IDOL™ Podcast: Instructional Design and Online Learning developer tips, tricks, advice, expert interviews, and insider information. It's the place where newbies come

Further Research and Resources

to learn and veterans share their knowledge. You can listen to this podcast wherever you get your podcasts.

IDOL courses Academy[SM]: The IDOL courses Academy[sm] is the only implementation program and pre-authorized trade school of its kind that not only shows you exactly how to create your job application assets and build a portfolio from scratch, but also includes credentials, mentorship, expert coaching, and paid experience opportunities in corporate instructional design and online learning for life! The IDOL courses Academy[sm] opens for enrollment four times a year. Enroll now or get on the waitlist.

IDOL™ courses Programs: Grab my hand, put your learning cap on, and prepare to get an in-depth how-to for everything instructional design and online learning. No matter where you're starting or what you want to focus on today, there is a program, course, or workbook that was designed especially for you. Here you will find descriptions of my most popular programs. Next to each description, you will see a button that will lead you to a page to either learn more about the program or to enroll and get started right away. Our programs are built by IDOLs for IDOLs.

Instructional Design Theories & Models

Following an instructional design model grounded in principles that connect to our best understanding of how people learn is essential to creating effective and engaging learning experiences that enable people to acquire and retain new knowledge and skills.

7 Instructional Design Theories and Models you NEED to know: These are the instructional design models you'll need to

281

know for an instructional design job interview in the corporate environment.

IDOL™ courses ID Models and Theories Videos: A full YouTube playlist all about the different instructional design theories and models.

Gagne's Nine Events of Instruction: Detailed blog post on the nine events of instruction by Robert Gagne.

Merrill's First Principles of Instruction: First Principles of Instruction provides a comprehensive instructional design model which is grounded in decades of research into the effective design of instruction.

ADDIE: As an instructional designer, you'll often hear the term ADDIE thrown around in job descriptions, articles, and videos about learning. This article is a quick starter guide to help you learn the ins and outs of the ADDIE framework.

SAM Model: SAM, which stands for the Successive Approximation Model, serves as an iterative design and delivery model to meet the immediate demands of usable training collateral.

Dick and Carey Instructional Design Model: The Dick and Carey Model is an instructional systems design (ISD) model taking a systems approach and based on the research of Walter Dick of Florida State University and Lou and James Carey of the University of South Florida.

Backward Design: Instructors typically approach course design in a "forward design" manner, meaning they consider the learning activities (how to teach the content), develop assessments around their learning activities, then attempt to

Further Research and Resources

draw connections to the learning goals of the course. In contrast, the backward design approach has instructors consider the learning goals of the course first.

The Kirkpatrick Model: This guide will introduce the Kirkpatrick Model and the benefits of using this model in your training program.

Andragogy: A champion of andragogy, self-direction in learning, and informal adult education, Malcolm S. Knowles was a very influential figure in the adult education field. Here we review his life and achievements, and assess his contribution.

Human-Centered Design: Human-centered design is a practical, repeatable approach to arriving at innovative solutions. Think of these methods as a step-by-step guide to unleashing your creativity, putting the people you serve at the center of your design process to come up with new answers to difficult problems.

Design Thinking Framework

Action Mapping: Action mapping is a streamlined process to design training in the business world.

Learning Strategies

Concrete Examples: This blog article explores what students remember from examples used in instruction.

Dual Coding: The dual coding learning strategy is all about using different learning materials in order to learn better. Dual coding is about combining verbal material with visuals in your teaching practice.

THE DO IT MESSY APPROACH

Elaboration: This blog article talks about the science of elaboration in learning. When students are asked a simple question, "why?," they strengthen the connective tissue around an idea, which builds knowledge.

Interleaving: Interleaving is a technique in which, instead of practicing a single skill over and over before moving on to learning the next skill, instructors mix or interleave several related skills together.

Retrieval Practice: Retrieval practice is a learning technique that simply asks students what they remember. Rather than cramming, reviewing, or re-teaching, retrieval practice encourages students to learn throughout an activity or exercise.

Spaced Practice: This is another alternative to cramming for an exam. Instead of spending a period of intense study just prior to an exam, spaced practice takes that same amount of time and spreads it out over several days, producing more long-lasting learning.

Self-Assessments: This paper focuses on two key aspects of self-evaluation in adult
education and training through the perspective of (a) a social cognitive framework which is used to categorize those factors that enhance self-efficacy and self-evaluation, and (b) the accuracy of self-evaluation.

Cognitive Load Theory: Educational psychologist, John Sweller, came up with this theory, which suggests that learning happens best when the instructional design aligns with the architecture of human cognition. Moving knowledge from short term to long term memory is a key aspect of making learning stick.

First Principles of Instruction

Summary of Merrill's First Principles of Instruction

Merrill's Principles Of Instruction: The Definitive Guide

M. David Merrill's Home Page

Visual Design

Mayer's 12 Principles

The 50 Most Important Rules of Document Design: Color CRAYON-TIP Method

Course Development Tools List

Storyboarding

Twinery: Branching scenario creator tool.

Milanote: Organization tool with storyboarding capabilities.

Boords: Storyboarding tool with easy sketches.

Storyboardthat: Video storyboarding tool with templates.

Miro: Concept mapping tool.

Mindmeister: Mind mapping tool.

THE DO IT MESSY APPROACH

Invision: Wireframing tool.

Job Aid Editing

Canva: All-round graphic design tool.

Visme: Canva alternative.

Ilovepdf: All sorts of tools for PDFs in one place.

PDF Escape: Make PDFs fillable for free.

Snagit: Advanced snipping tool.

Inkscape: Free Adobe Illustrator alternative.

Affinity: Adobe Illustrator alternative.

Kami: Annotate PDFs.

Video and Animation

Camtasia: The industry-standard video editing tool.

Audacity: Record and edit your voiceover or soundtracks.

Screencast-O-Matic: Free video editing tool for Mac.

Biteable: Video maker with templates.

Powtoon: Video maker with templates.

Playposit: Add interactivity to videos.

Animaker: Video maker with templates.

Vyond: Animation editor with professional templates.

Renderforest: Video maker with templates.

Moovly: Video maker with templates.

My SimpleShow: Video maker with templates.

Meme Generator: Create free memes.

Iorad: Rapid software tutorial generator.

Presentation Tools

Genial.ly: Create interactive presentations.

Prezi: Create interactive presentations.

Keynote: iOS presentation tool.

Google Forms: Create a quick survey or a quiz.

Typeform: A fancy version of Google Forms.

Nearpod: Make slides interactive.

Kahoot: Live quizzing.

Mentimeter: Live interactive slides.

Wooclap: Live interactive slides.

THE DO IT MESSY APPROACH

Aha slides: Live interactive slides.

Poll Everywhere: Create live polls to encourage learner interaction.

Crowdpurr: Live interaction tool.

Padlet: Collaboration tool.

ManyCam: Create visually interesting video presentations.

eLearning Development

H5P: Empowers everyone to create, share, and reuse interactive content.

Articulate 360 (Rise + Storyline): Supports eLearning developers in every step of the course authoring process.

iSpring: Tools for creating interactive online courses and assessments.

Adapt: Responsive eLearning design tool.

Adobe Captivate: Digital learning solutions.

Lectora Inspire: Digital learning solutions.

Easy Generator: Cloud-based eLearning authoring tool.

Gomo: Cloud-based eLearning authoring tool.

Evolve Authoring: Cloud-based eLearning authoring tool.

Further Research and Resources

IsEasy: An eLearning toolkit.

Construct: Tool for creating games to enhance learning.

Ed app: Tool for creating mobile-friendly, minicourses.

7Taps: Tool for creating microlearning courses for any device.

EduFlow: eLearning platform with tools and a community.

DominKnow: eLearning authoring tool.

CourseArc: Content authoring and management system.

Xerte Online Toolkit: Suite of browser-based eLearning development tools.

Elucidat: eLearning authoring tool.

Text/Speech/Subtitles

Otter: Speech to text transcription tool.

Natural Readers: Text to speech AI tool.

Well Said Lab: Text to speech AI tool.

Amazon Polly: Text to speech AI tool.

Speechelo: Text to speech AI tool.

Descript: All-in-one audio and video editing, as easy as a doc.

THE DO IT MESSY APPROACH

Accessibility Tools

Authoring Tools Guidelines: Guidelines for accessibility for digital courses.

Color blindness generator: See your course through the eyes of someone colorblind.

Color contrast checker: For the visually impaired, the lack of contrast on websites can be an issue. This site checks the contrast on your course.

Example Courses

Counterfeit Bill Identification by Justin Morello

Sweet Dreams: Fundamentals of Sleep Hygiene by Lina Jurkunas

Going Up? Let Your Elevator Speech Take You to the Top! by Holli Prior

A Quick Guide to Podcast Formats by Rudi Osman

Counterfeit Caper by Brian Harris

Remote Communication by Ruth Crossman

Food Allergies by Ivett Csordas

Summer Vegetable Garden by Brooklyn McPherson

Filing Status Tax Prep by Fe'Dricka Moore

SCRUM Team by Thao Nguyen

Counting Macros by Sari Bailey

Cybersecurity Awareness by Ashley Dresser

Recycling by Mariam Baassiri

Feedback by Jennifer Sweet

FTD: A Devastating Disease (great storytelling) by Margaret Bowling

Wash Your Hair by Gretchen Johanson

Phishing Quiz Interactions by Jigsaw

Home Visit Skills Practice by Serious Learning

How to Fight a Bear by Slide Sugar

Robot Simulation Training by Universal Robots

Active Listening in the Workplace by Giulia Pizzi

Our World War by the BBC Studio

How to Change a Tire by Adriana Persellin

Giving Feedback in the Workplace by Raul Fajardo

Student Portfolios

IDOL courses Academy student portfolios

Resources in the Book

Merrill, M. D. (2009). "First Principles of Instruction." In C. M. Reigeluth & A. Carr (Eds.), Instructional Design Theories and Models: Building a Common Knowledge Base (Vol. III). New York: Routledge Publishers.

Merrill, M. D. (2013). *First Principles of Instruction: Identifying and Designing Effective, Efficient, and Engaging Instruction*. San Francisco: Pfeiffer, A Wiley Imprint.

22 Questions: Your Quick & Dirty Needs Analysis

FURTHER READING

Like the book? Take the course!

Praise for the IDOL courses Academy[SM]:

"There are so many great resources in IDOL courses Academy[SM], but the most helpful one for me is the community of peers and professionals that give constructive feedback on your portfolio. Everyone whom I have received feedback from has been very helpful and kind. I feel confident that IDOL courses Academy[SM] will continue to be a valuable resource for me as I grow more in my career!" -Samuel Monroe

"Without the IDOL courses Academy[SM], I would not have made it this far. The resources, support, and information I learned are priceless. This is such a worth self-investment. I am an IDOL[TM] fan for life!" -Fe'Dricka Moore

"The IDOL courses Academy[SM] was the best investment I've ever made in myself. I knew in 2018 that I wanted to pursue Instructional Design but had no experience. I attended an online certification program and while it put me in the right direction, I was no closer to my goals. Then, in August 2020, I learned about the IDOL courses Academy[SM]. I immediately began researching it and after meeting with Robin, I made the leap. The change in my abilities in the last five months is incredible. I feel so much more confident and that is a result of the deliberate practice and the feedback system in place. Even during the job search,

THE DO IT MESSY APPROACH

Robin and other coaches helped me with questions I had until I finally reached my goal of landing a job. In five months I went from going nowhere in my ID journey to landing a position with a prestigious learning company in my area." -Adam Briggs

"The IDOL courses Academy^{SM} helped me feel more confident about my knowledge, perfect the industry lingo, see more of what's getting done out there, start building an actual portfolio and decide what parts of instructional design and eLearning development spoke to me the most. The support of the mentors and other members continues to be invaluable!" -Maria Teixeira

ABOUT THE AUTHOR

ROBIN SARGENT PHD, IS AN entrepreneur, instructional designer, and former professor, recognized as a leader in the instructional design community. She is the Owner and Founder of IDOL courses, IDOL Talent, and VITAL courses. IDOL courses is the trade school that serves clients through IDOL Talent while developing the next generation of creative learning designers. *Business Insider* heralds the IDOL courses Academy[SM] as "one of the best choices out there if you're serious about starting a career in corporate instructional design, but don't want to pay for a master's degree."

Earning her PhD in Education with a specialization in instructional design and online learning, she has coached, mentored, and taught thousands of current and aspiring learning designers. Her dissertation was on the gamification of corporate training, and her vision is to create an IDOL world for all learners.

Dr. Robin is also a former Director of Learning & Development for a billion-dollar staffing firm with over 17 years of corporate instructional design experience. She serves as a volunteer board member for DESIGNxHUMANITY, a design collective and apprenticeship program pairing experienced creatives with fresh faces to collaborate on real-world projects advocating for Black, Indigenous, and People of Color. In addition, she

THE DO IT MESSY APPROACH

started the IDOL World project to match non-profit organizations with access to instructional designers and free eLearning modules on relevant topics. Robin lives in Atlanta with her husband, Kris, and their three boys.

Connect with Dr. Robin Sargent:

Website: www.idolcourses.com
Trade School: www.idolcourses.com/academy
LinkedIn: https://www.linkedin.com/in/robinsargent/
Facebook: https://www.facebook.com/IDOLcourses/
Instagram: https://www.instagram.com/idolcourses
Email: info@idolcourses.com

Printed in Great Britain
by Amazon